MANDALA COLORING BOOK

The World's Best Mandala Coloring Book

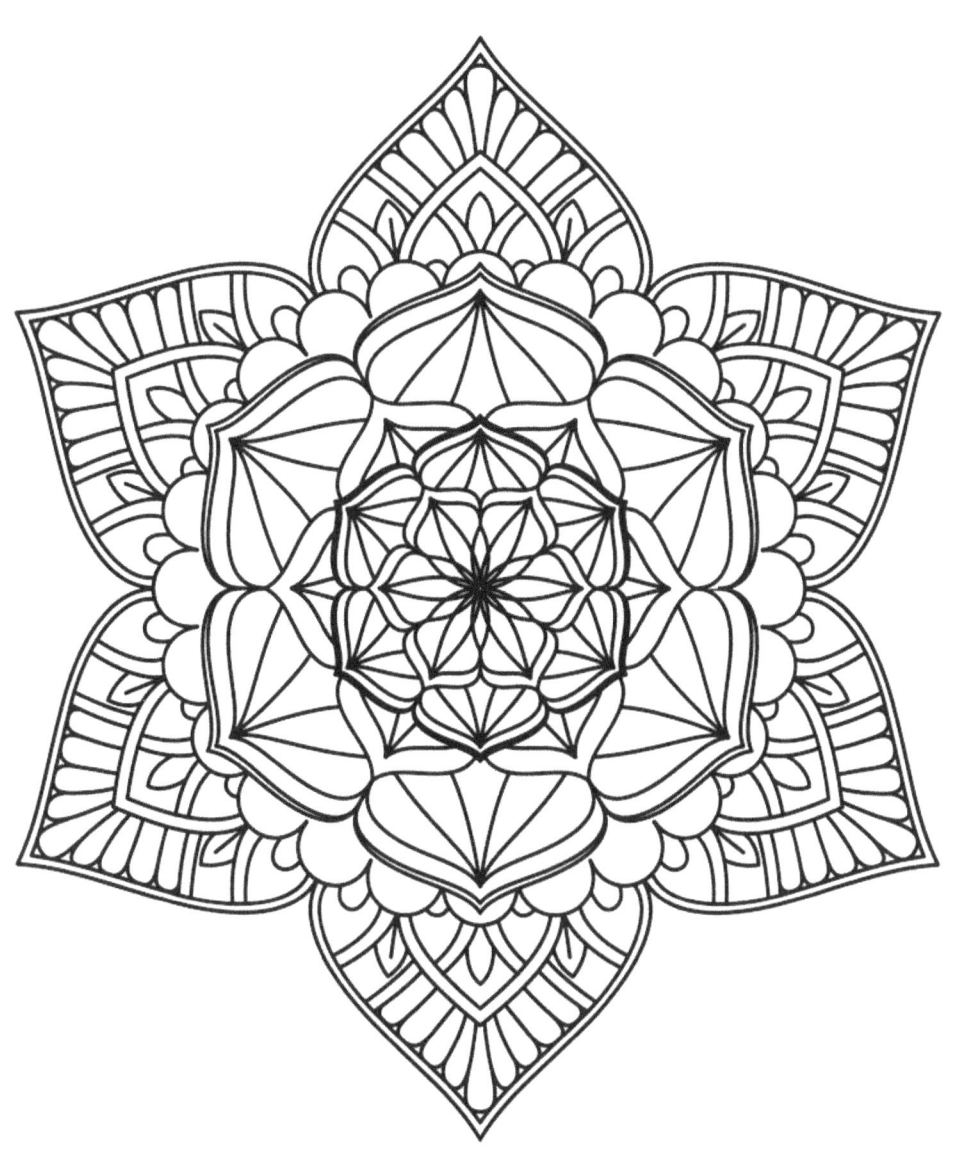

This book belongs to:

_____

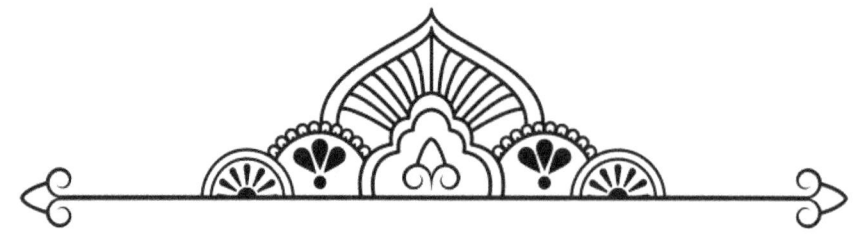

Let this book help you find the balance of your life through creativity.

Choose one or more mandala per day and color it using whatever medium you have. May it be colored pencils, markers, watercolor, pastels, etc.

Be absorbed in the moment and release stress and tension.

Focus on coloring and relaxation.

Happy coloring!!!

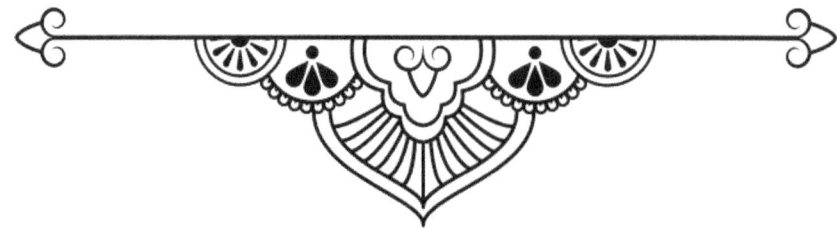

Cut and use this as your page blotter.

Put it below the page of your chosen mandala to prevent any inks or colors to bleed into the other pages below it.

Happy coloring!!!

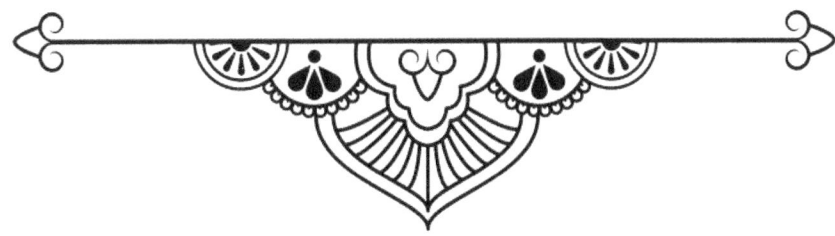

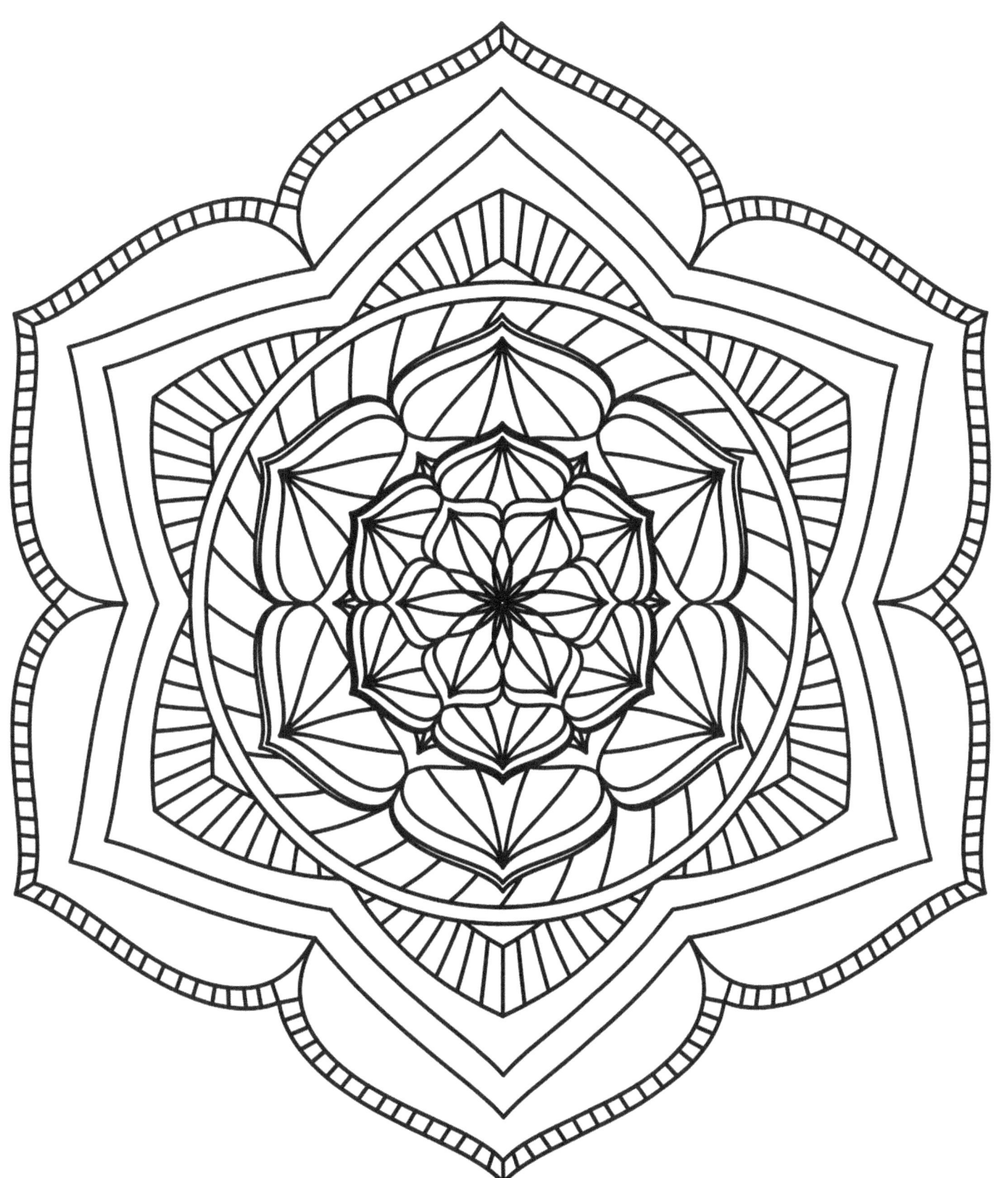

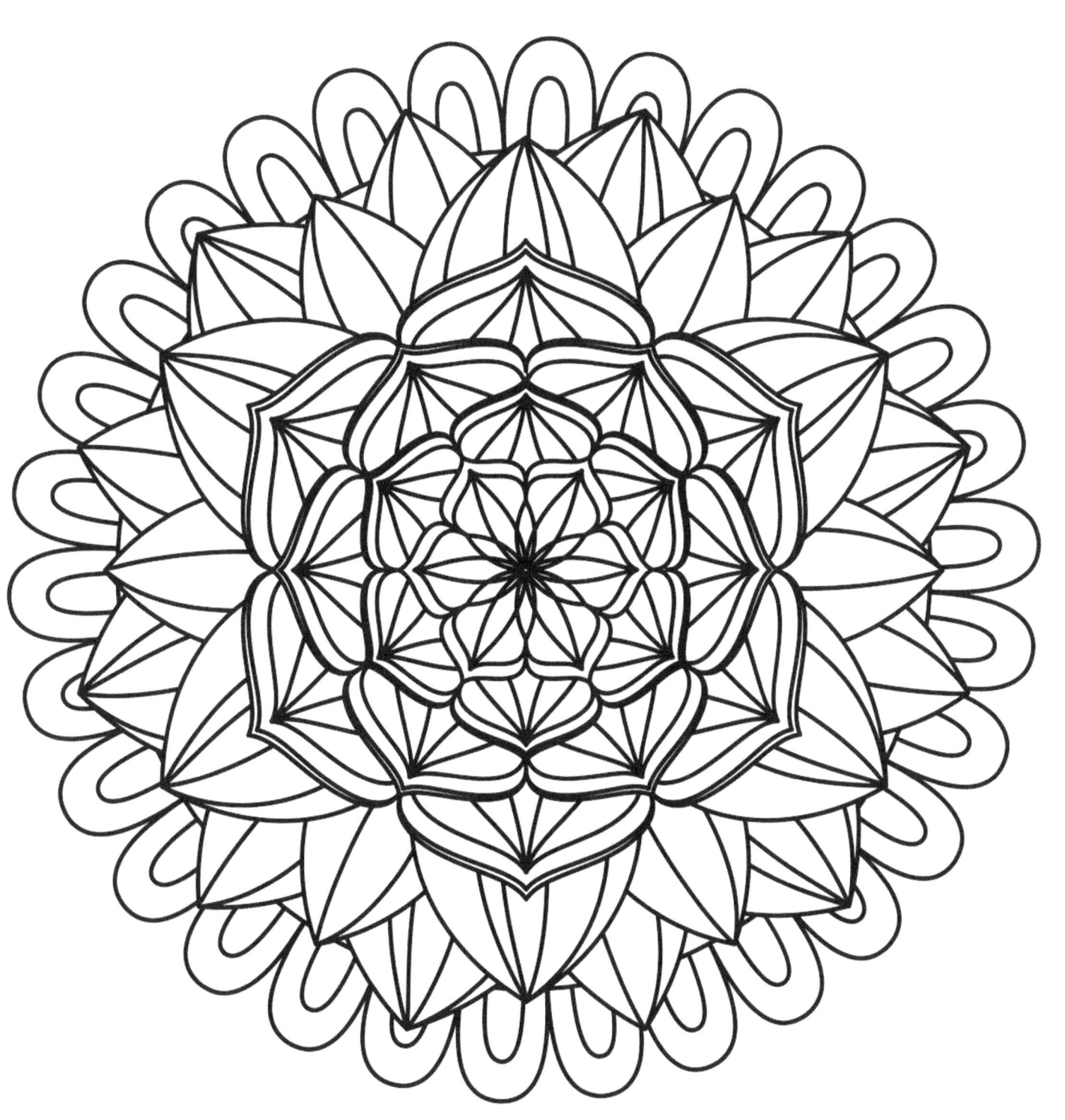

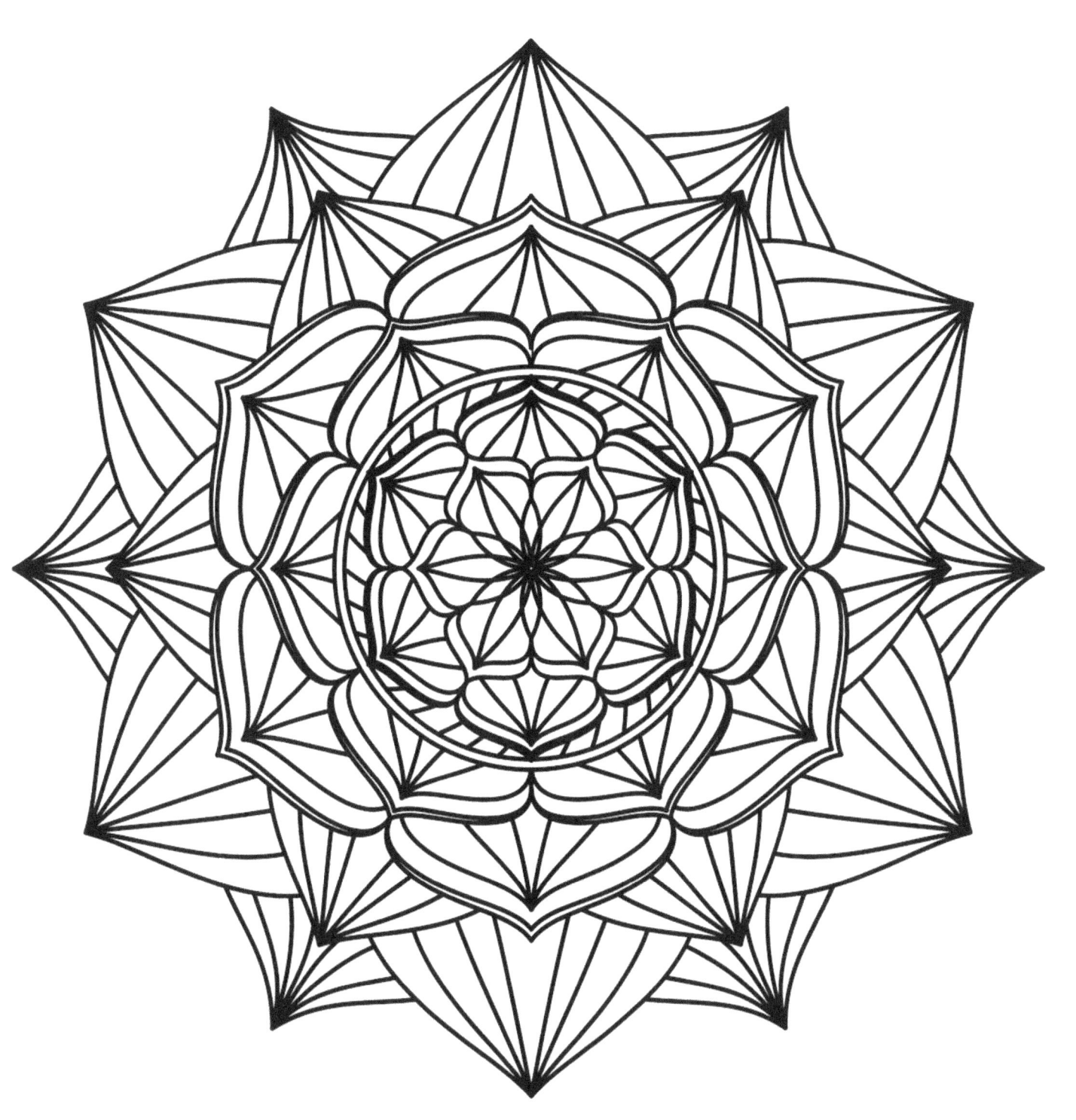

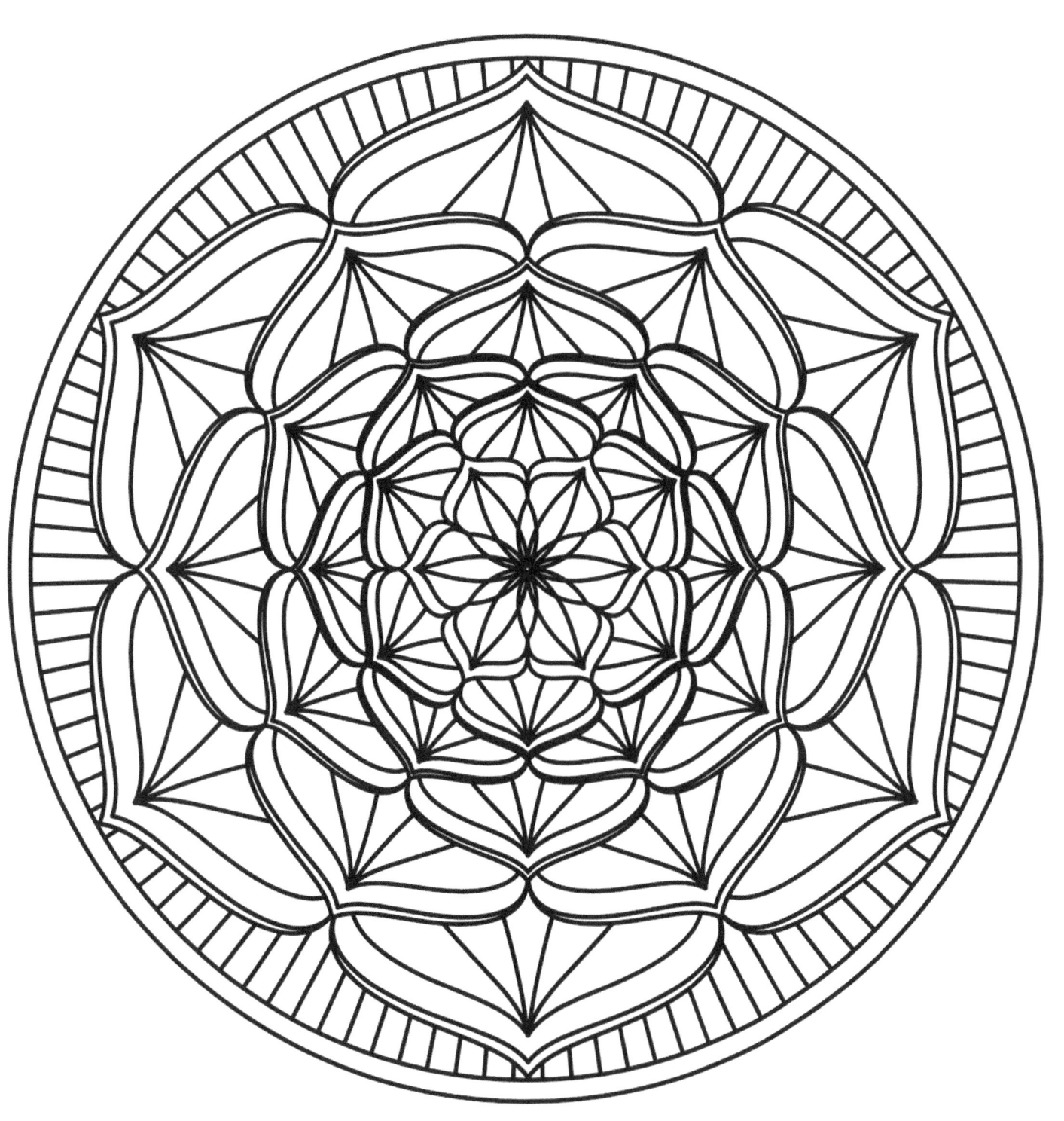

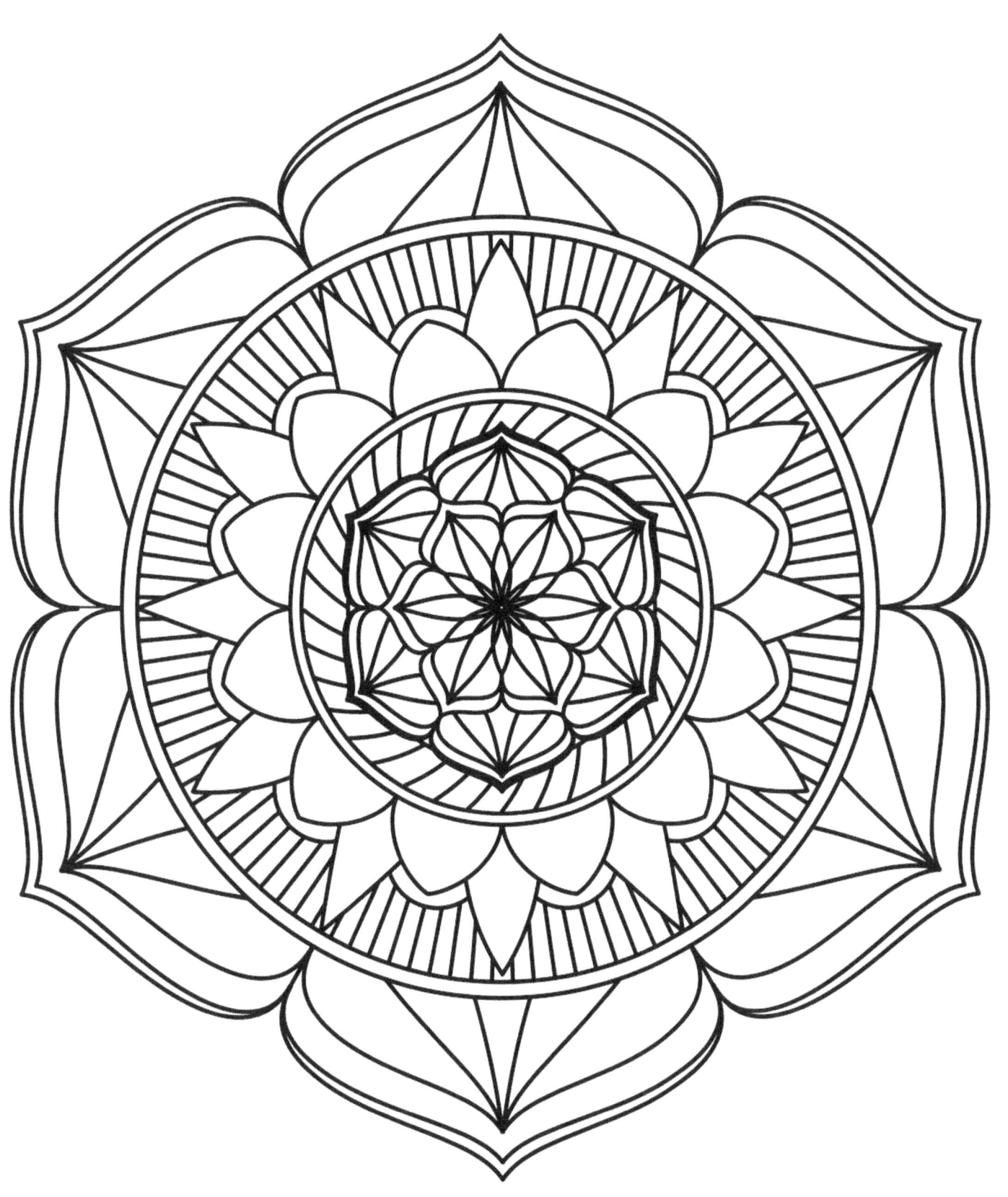

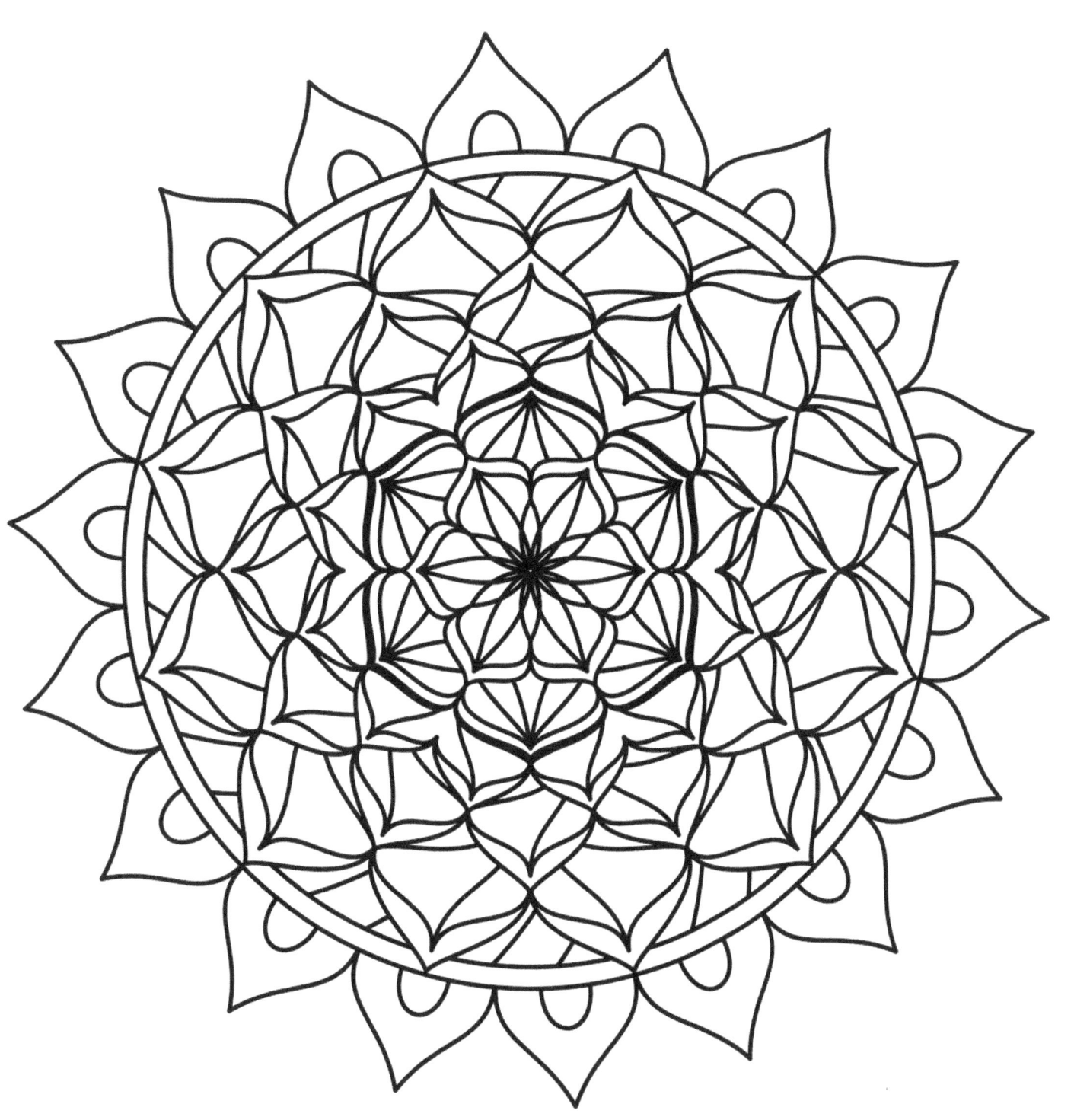

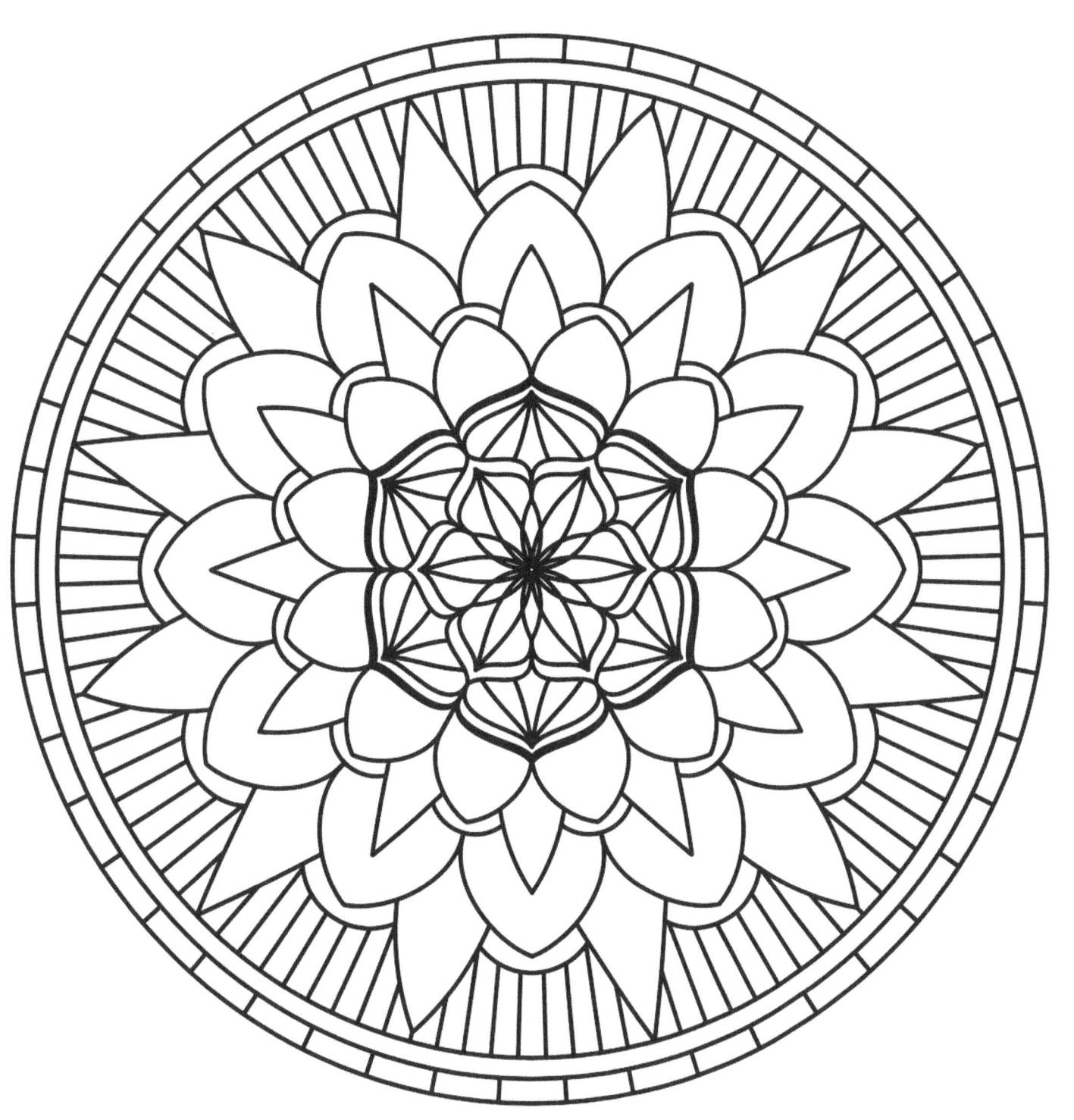

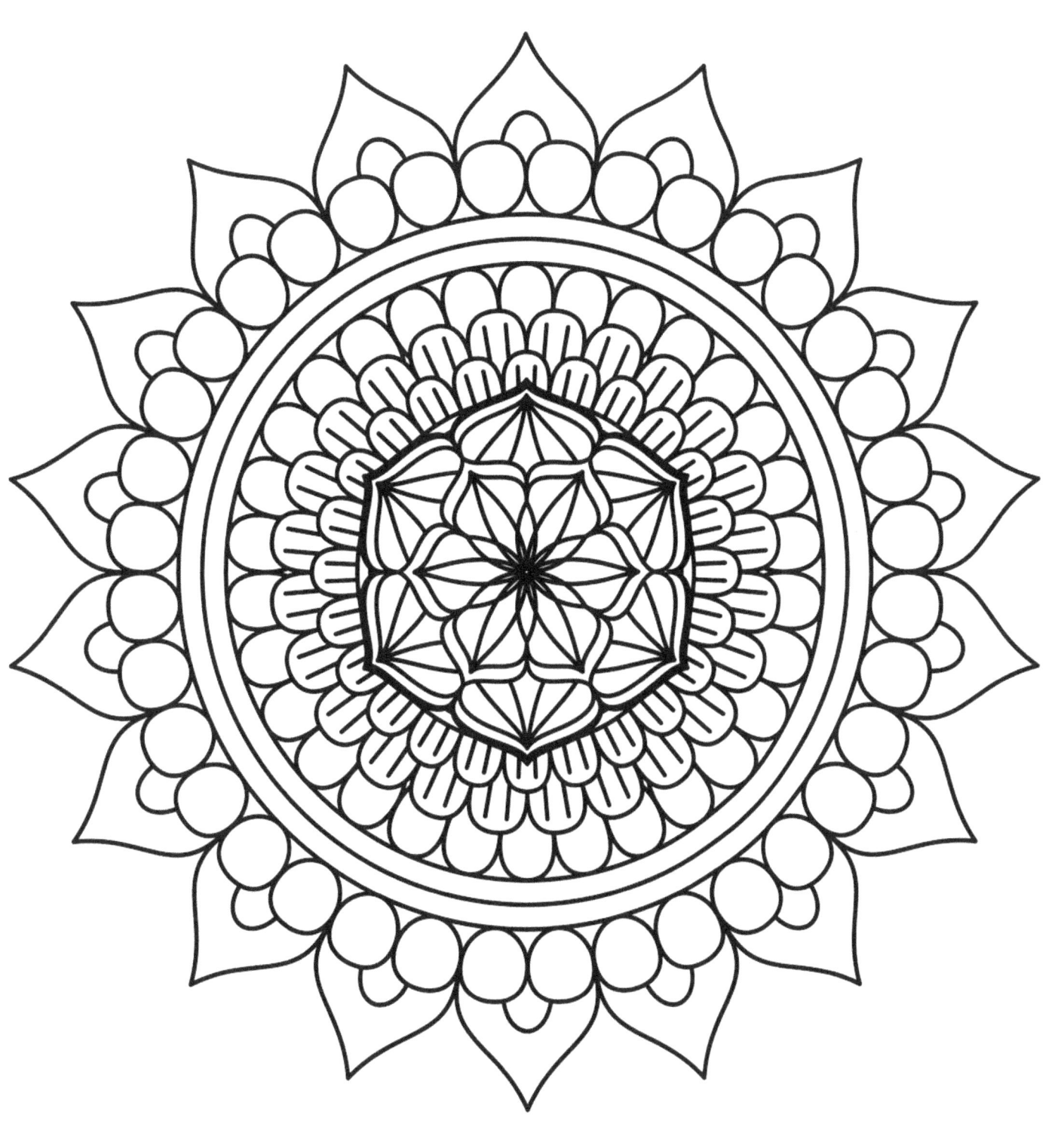

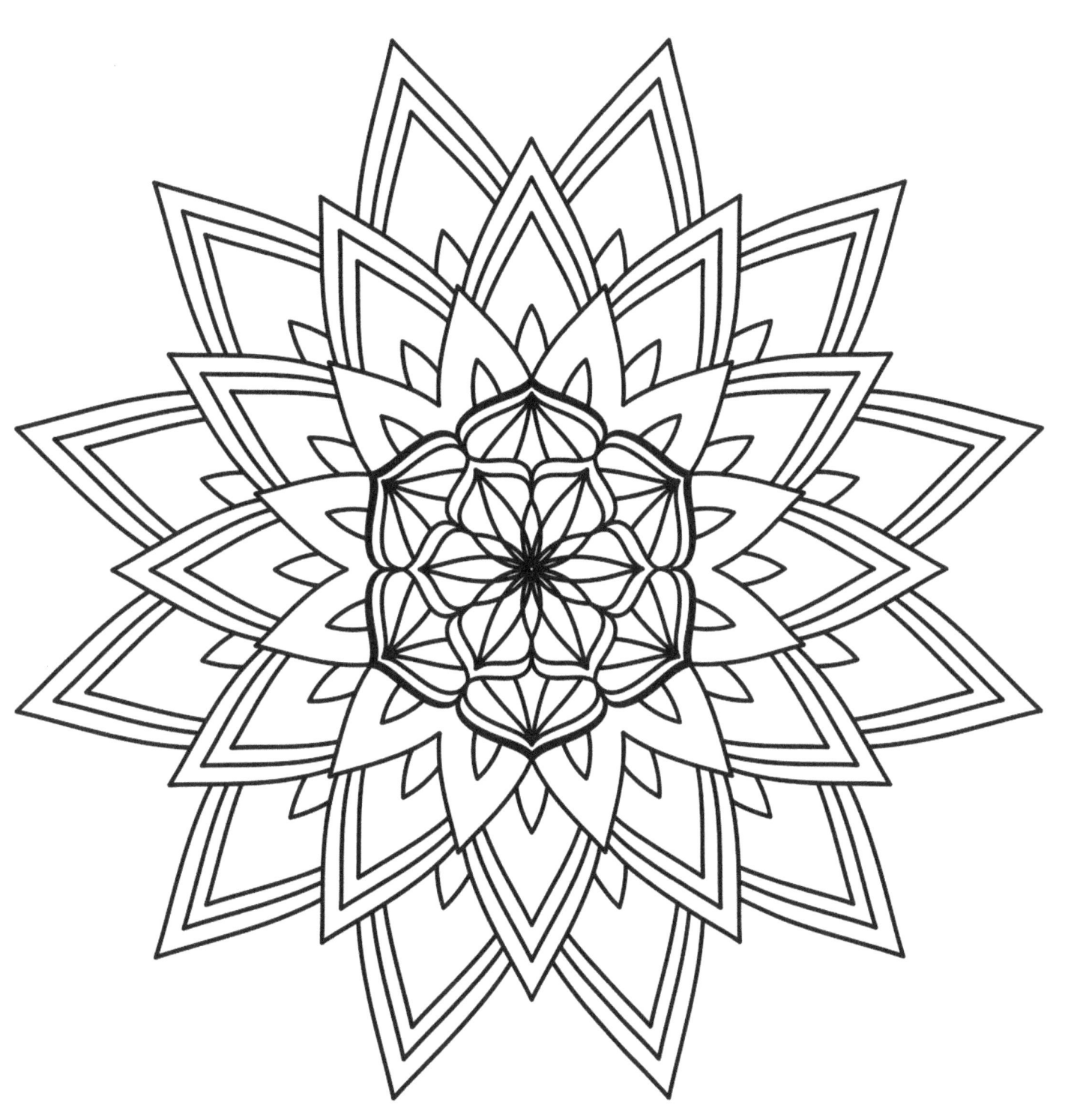

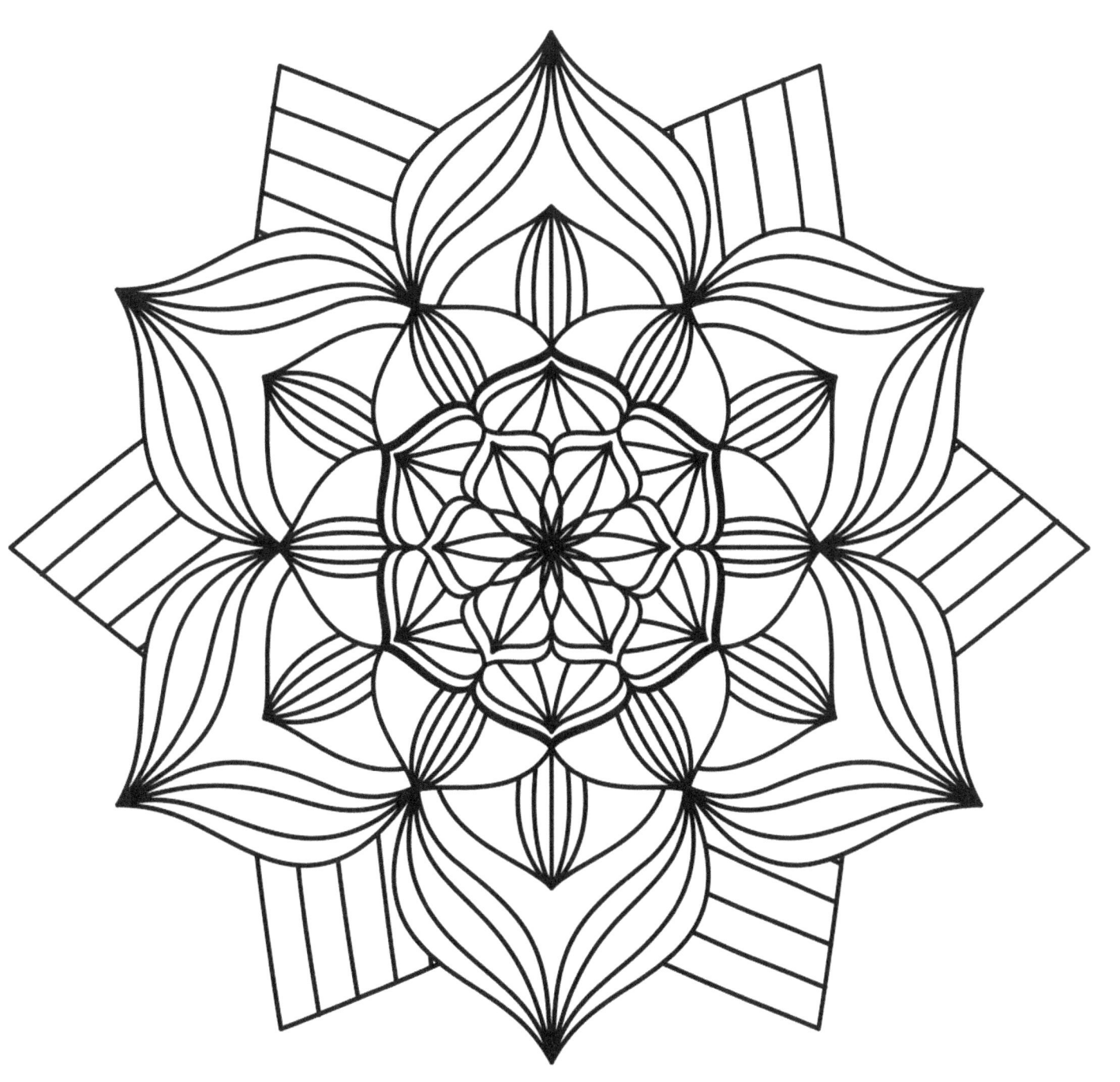

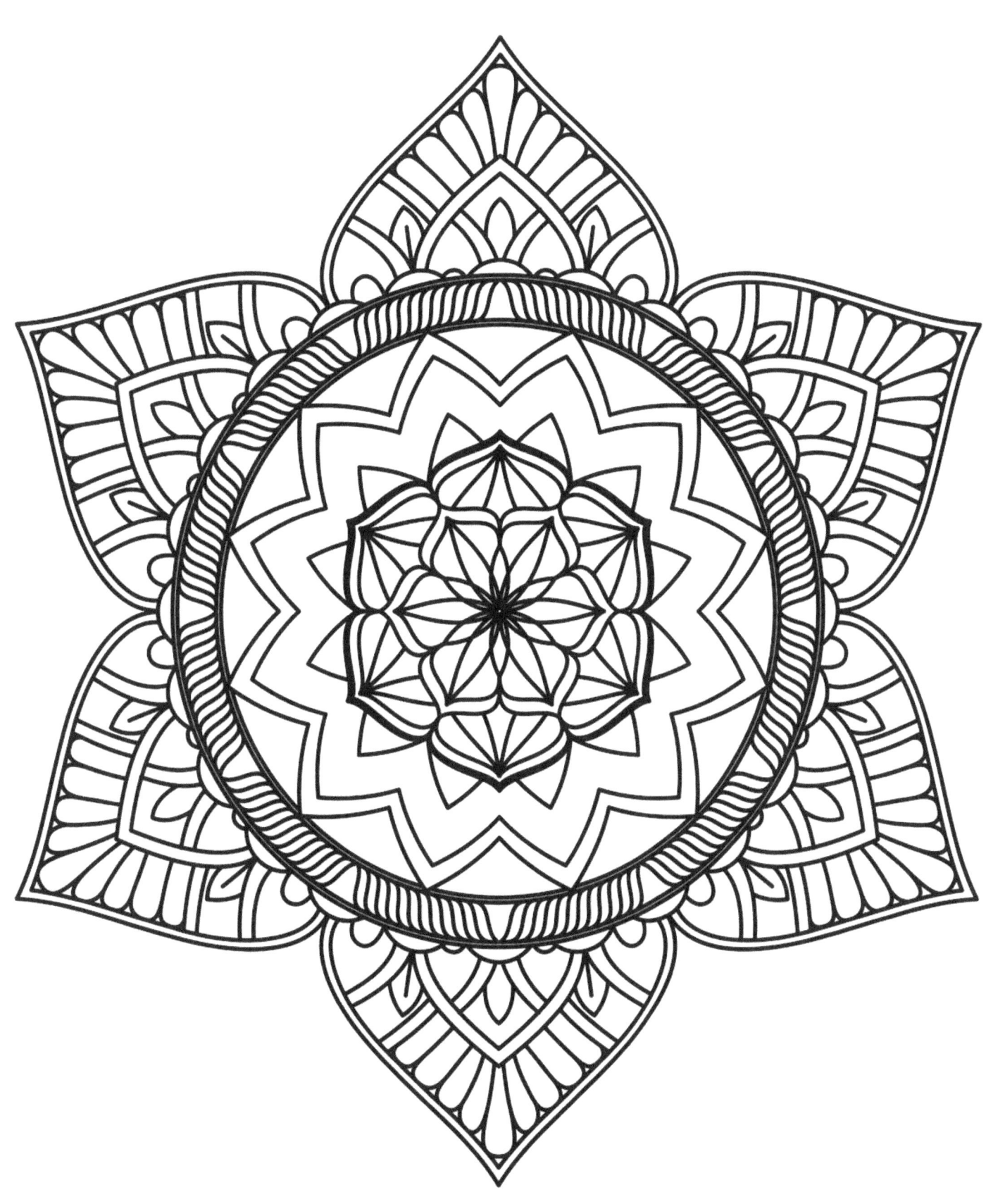

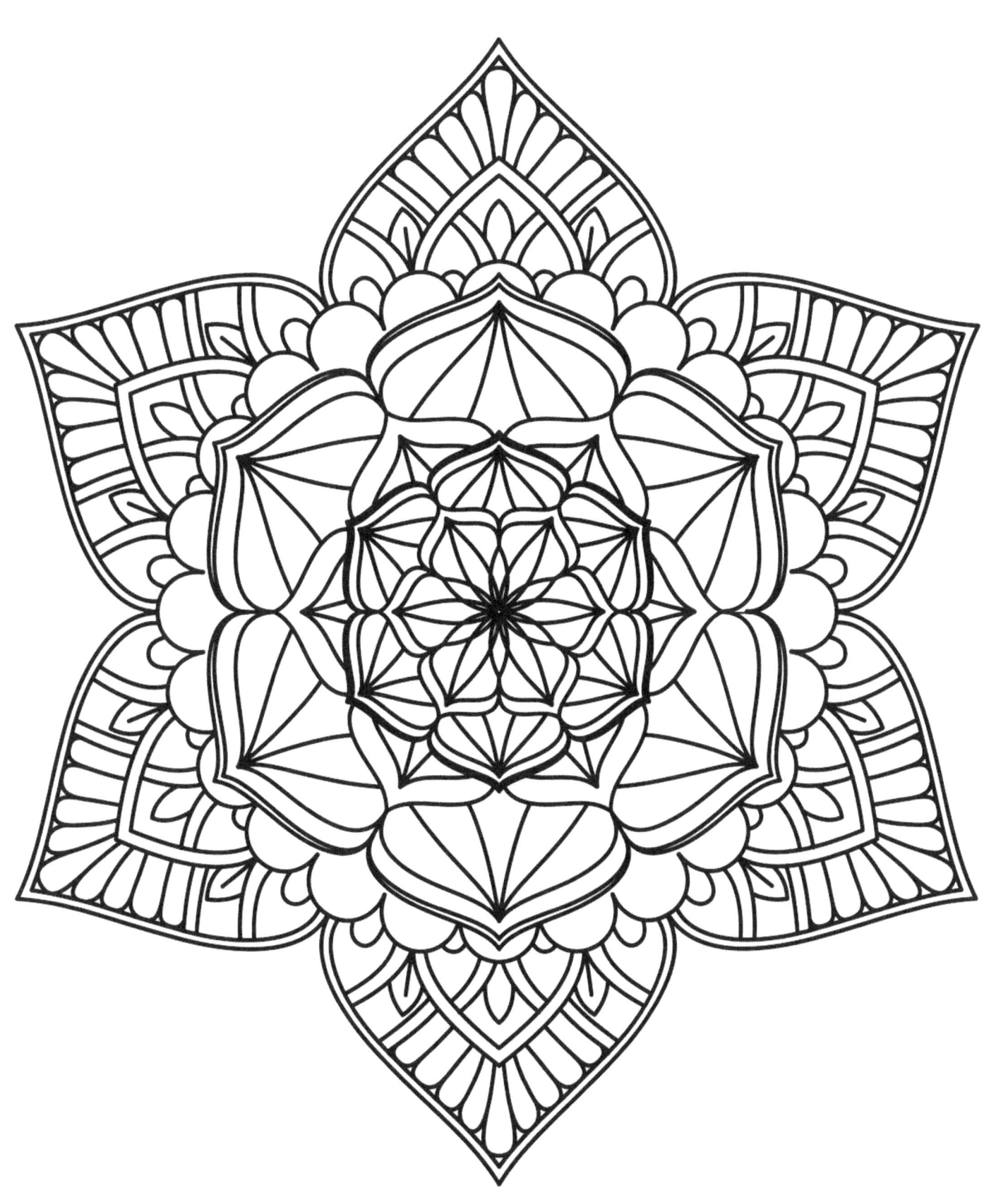

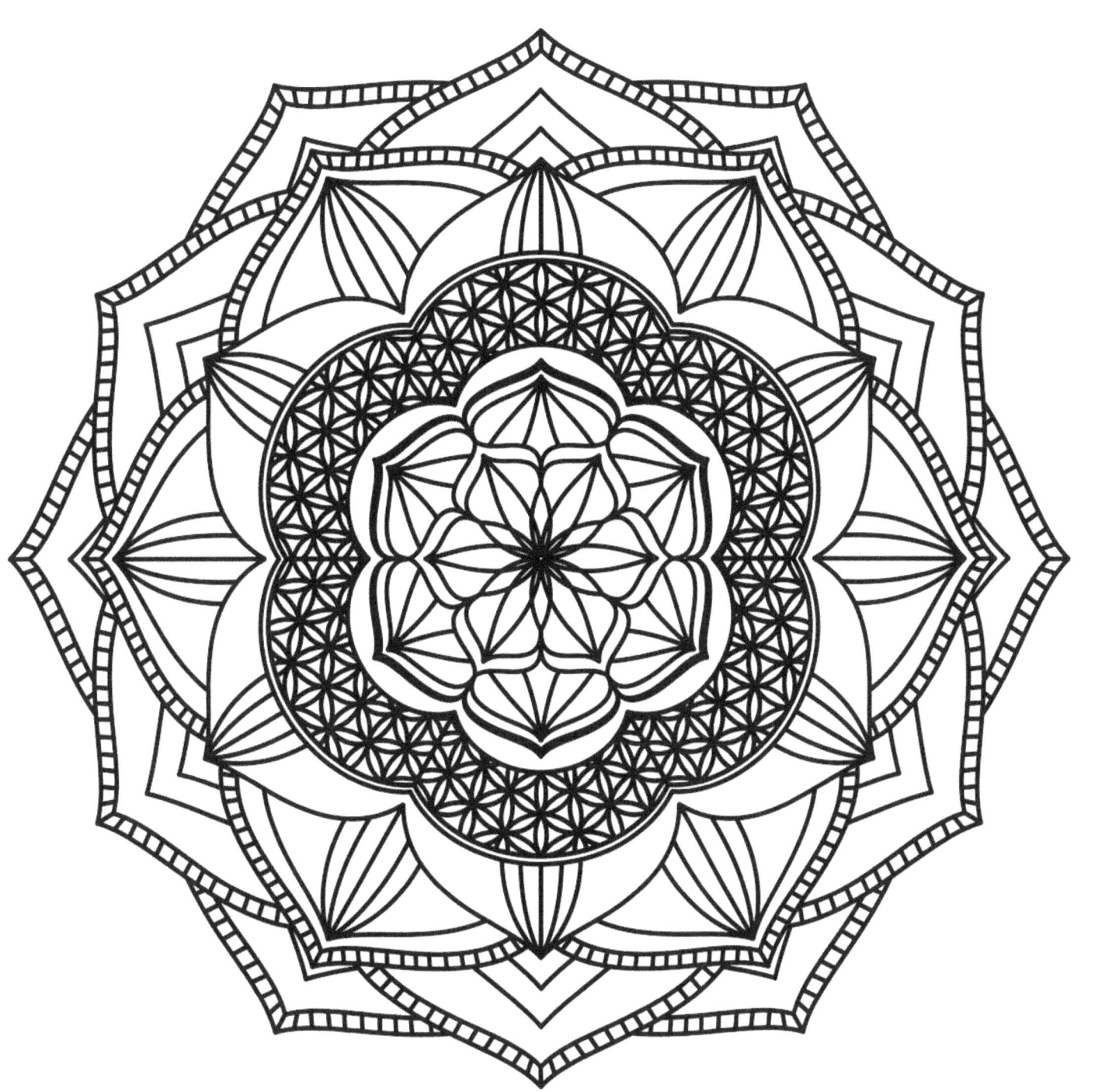

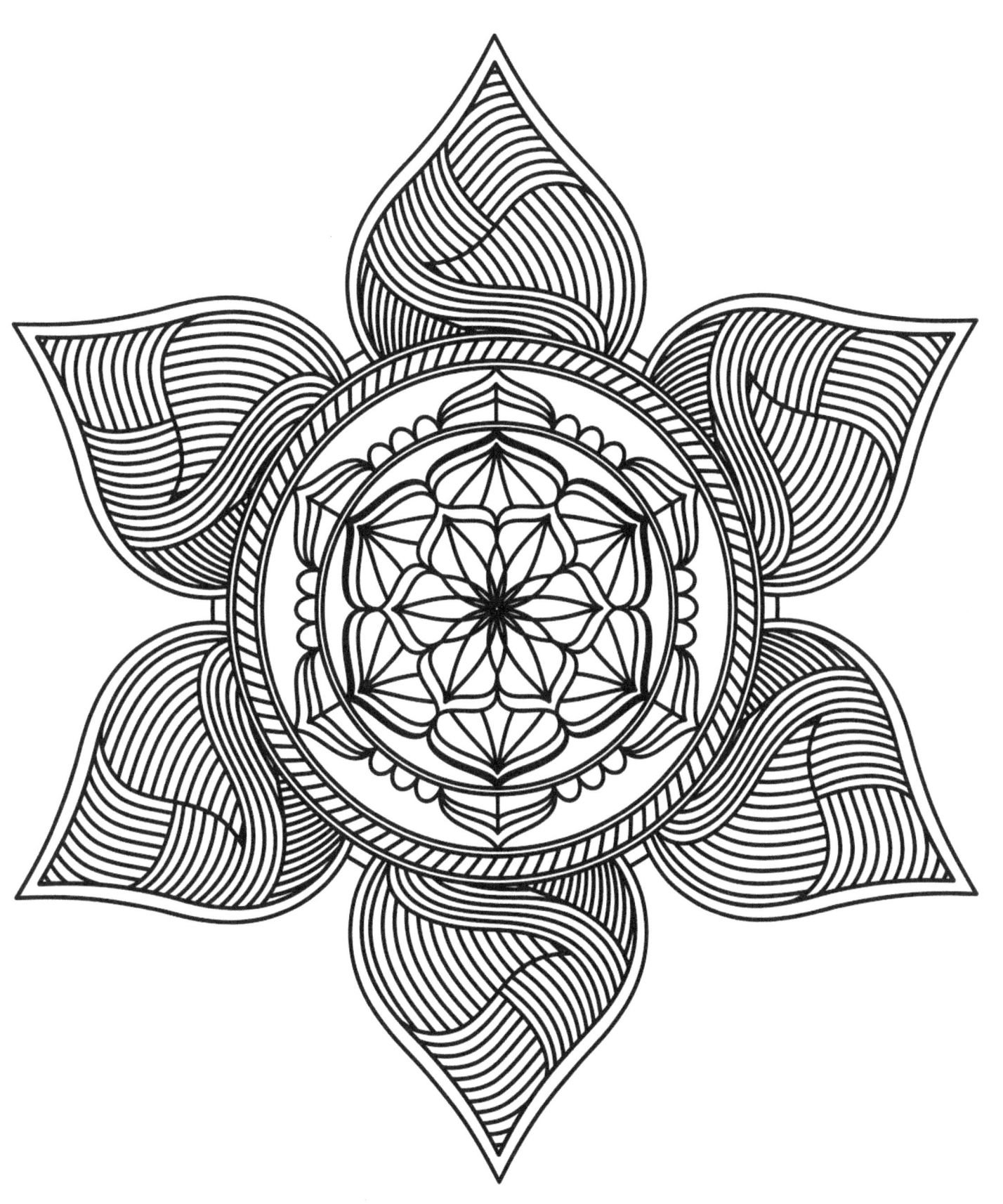

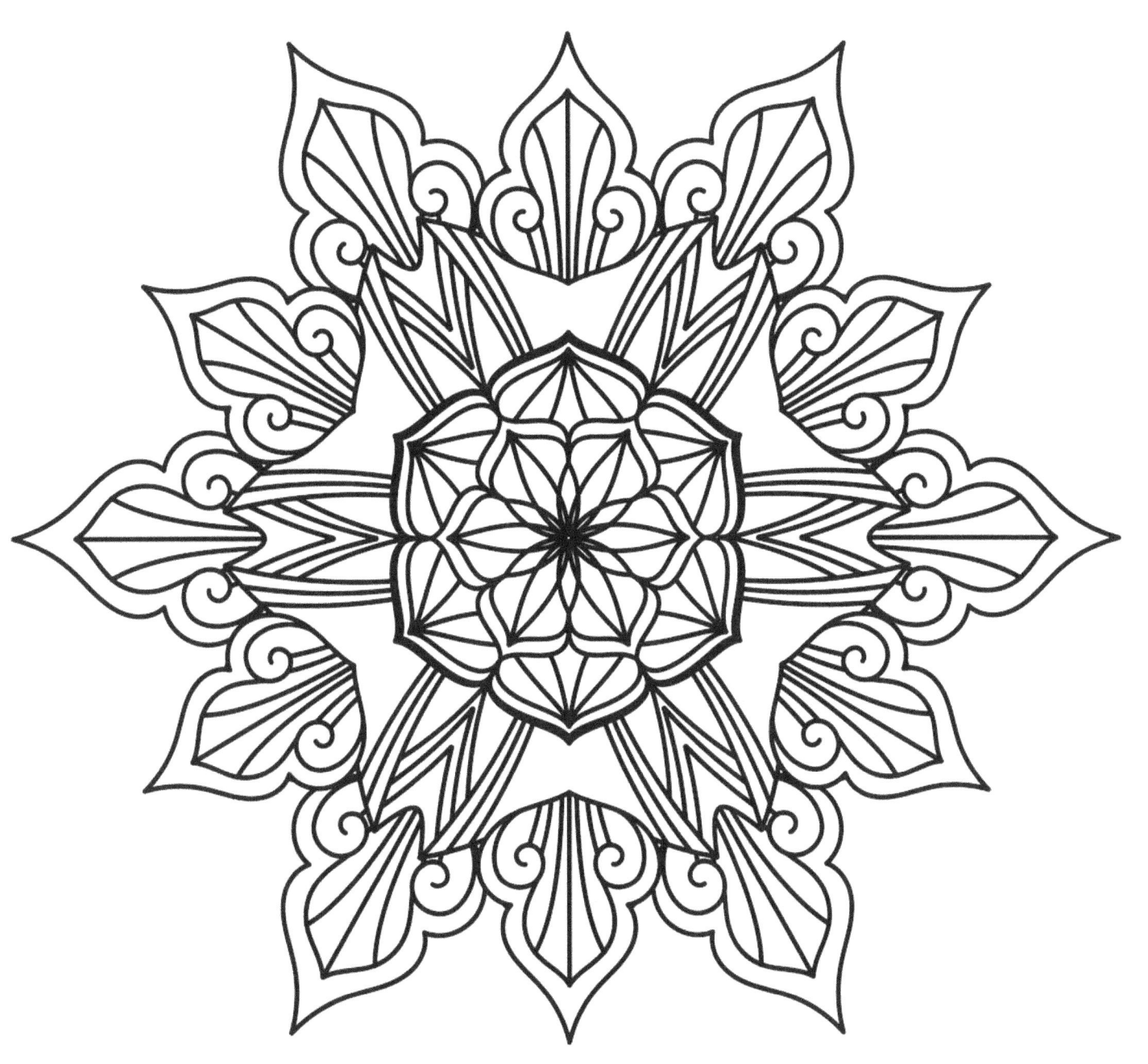

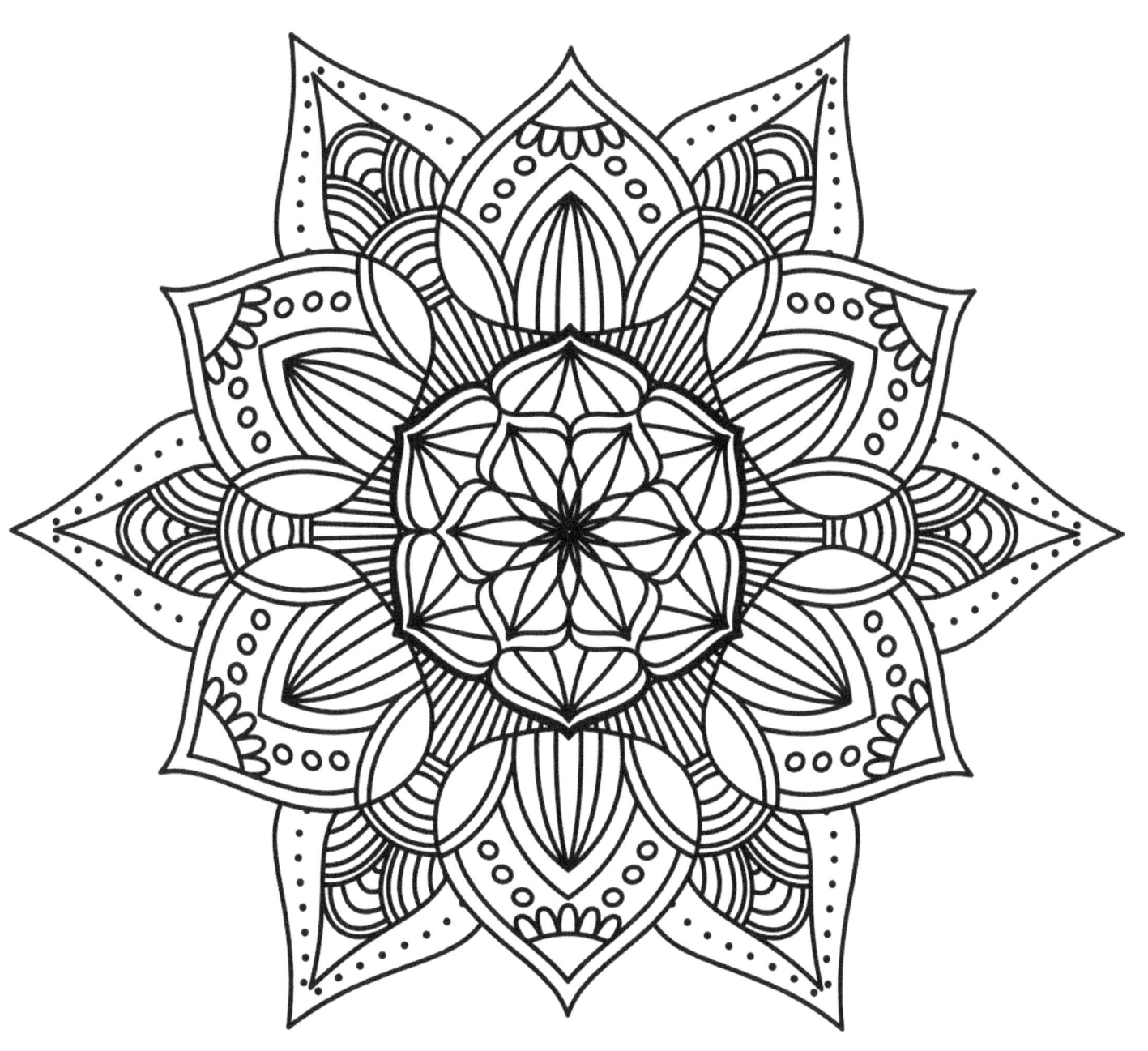

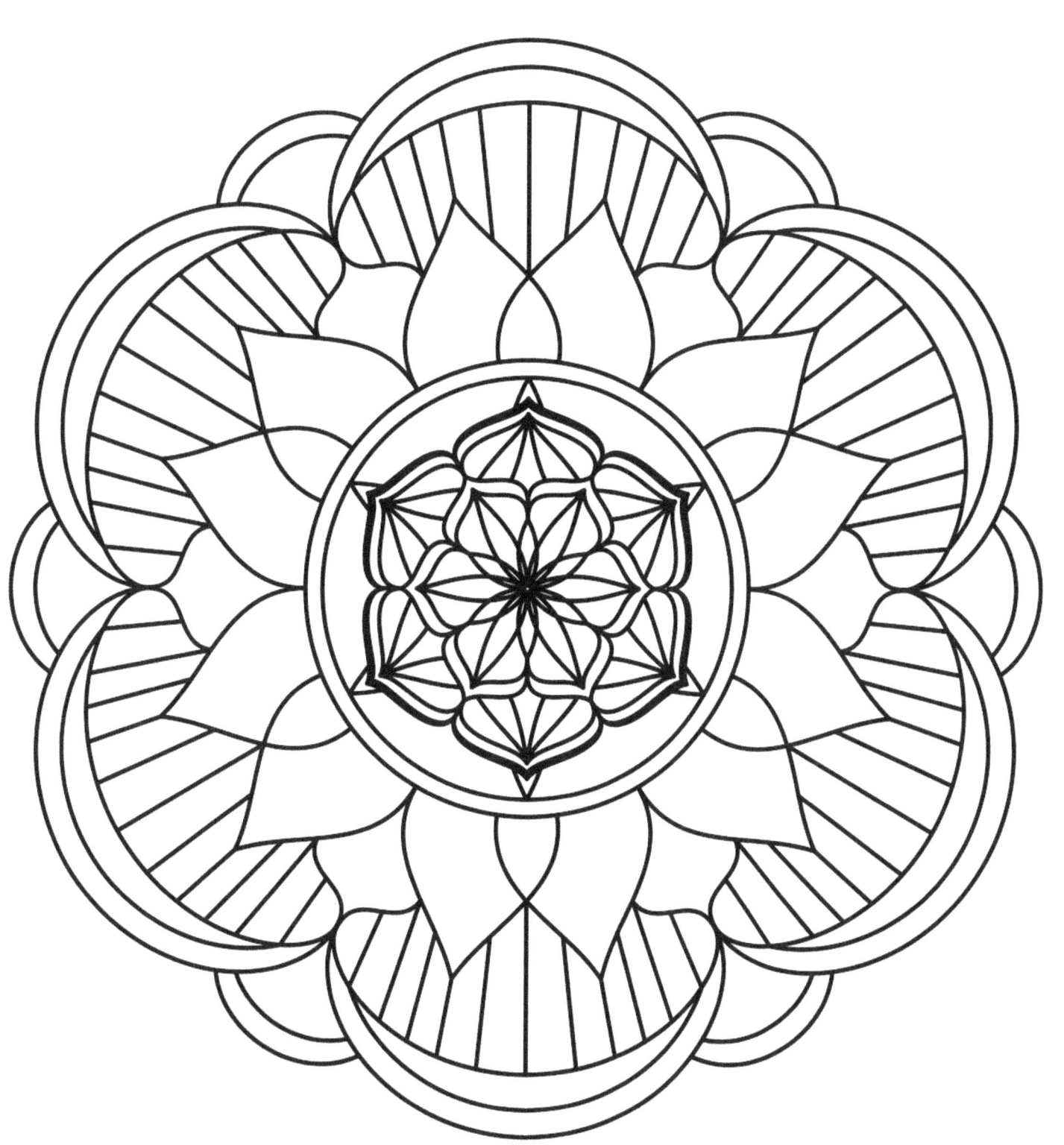

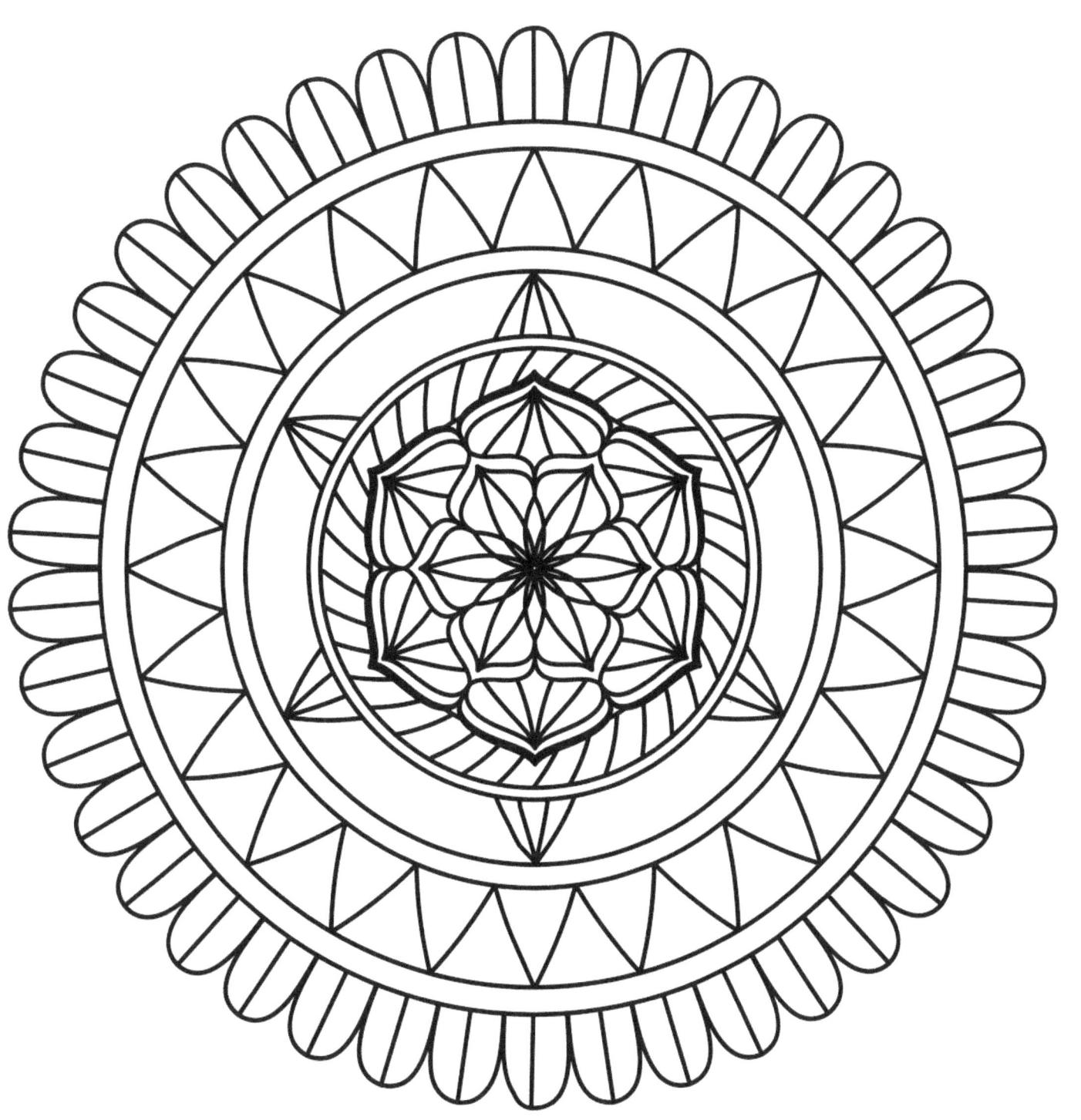

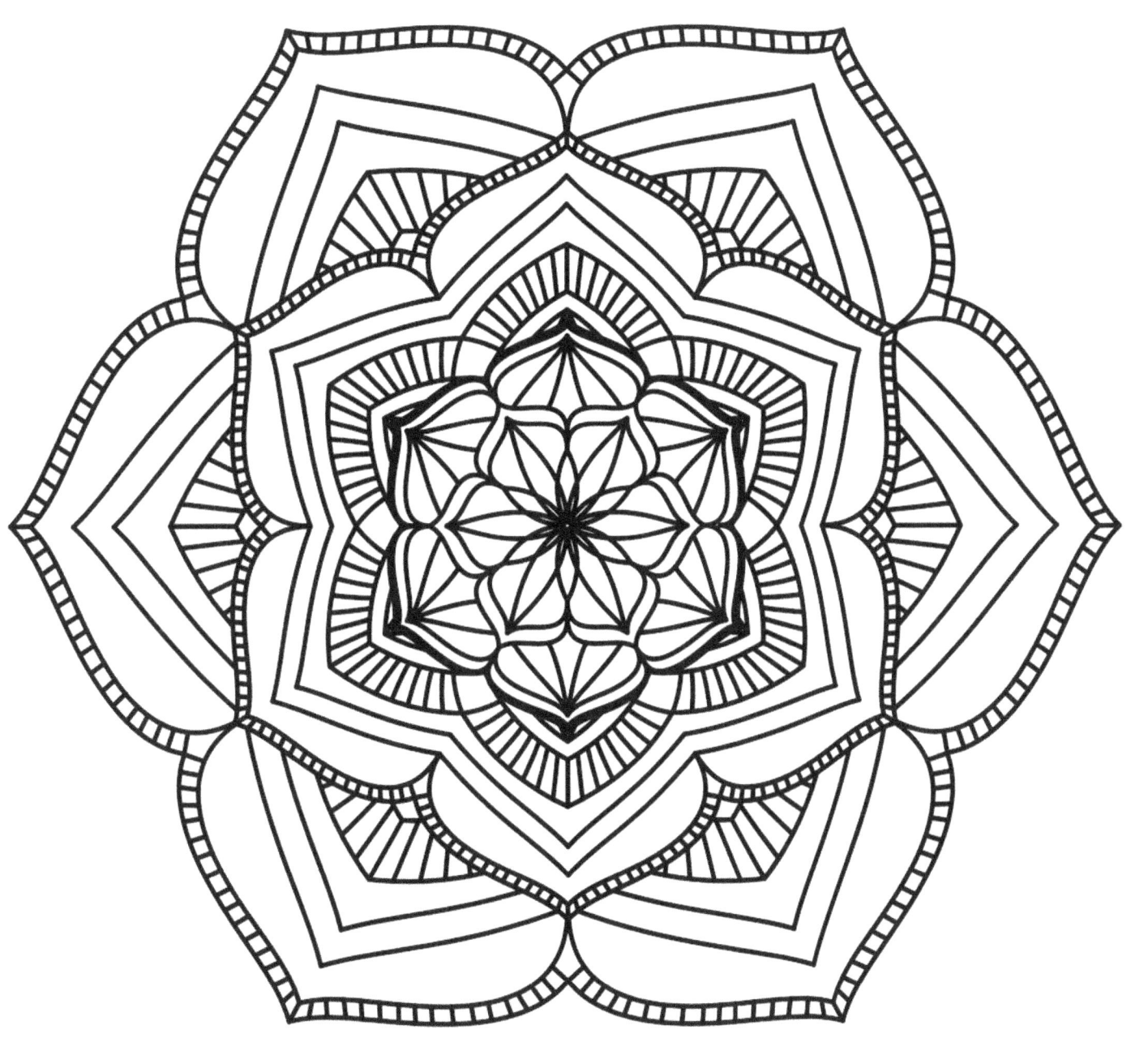

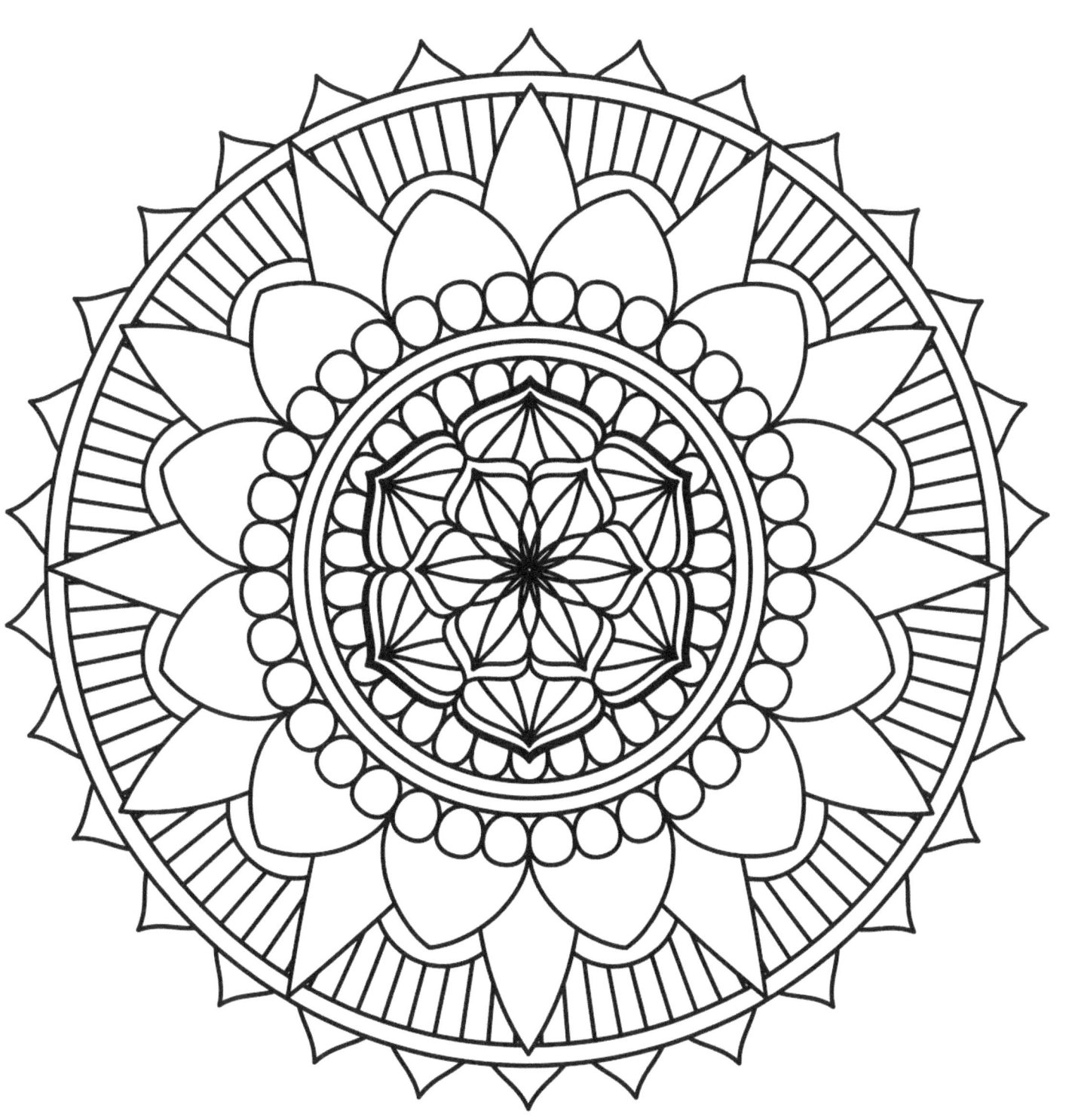

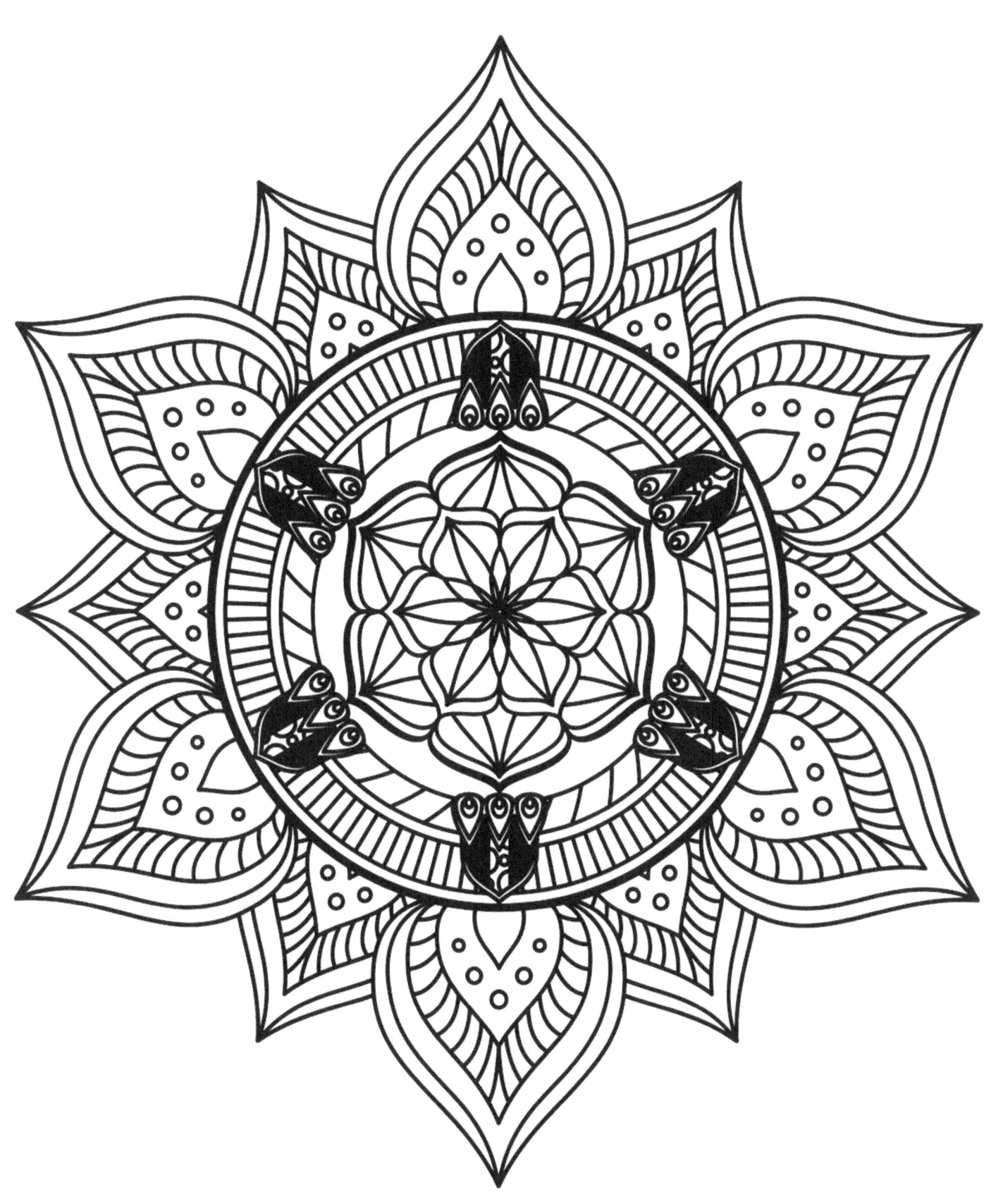

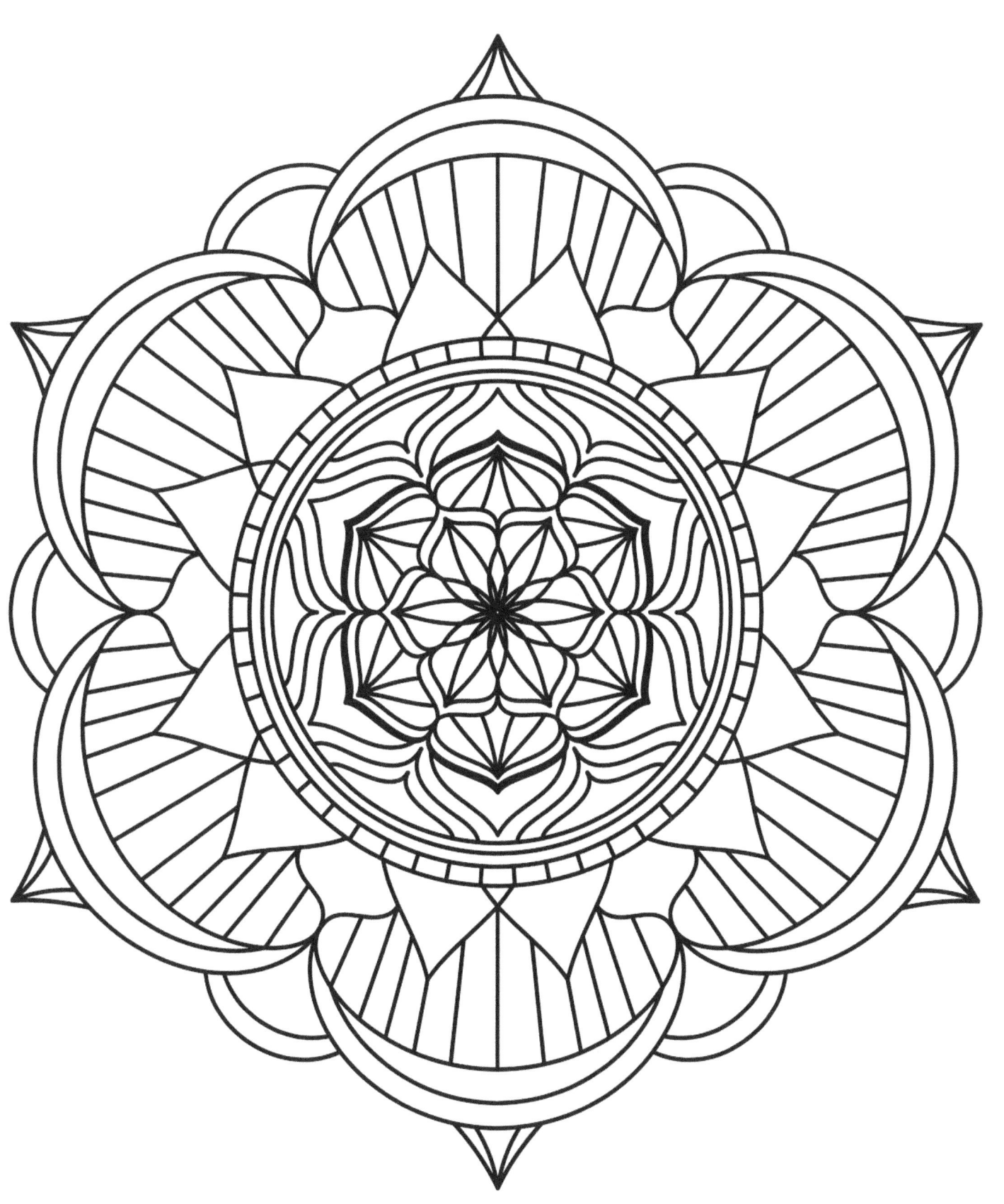

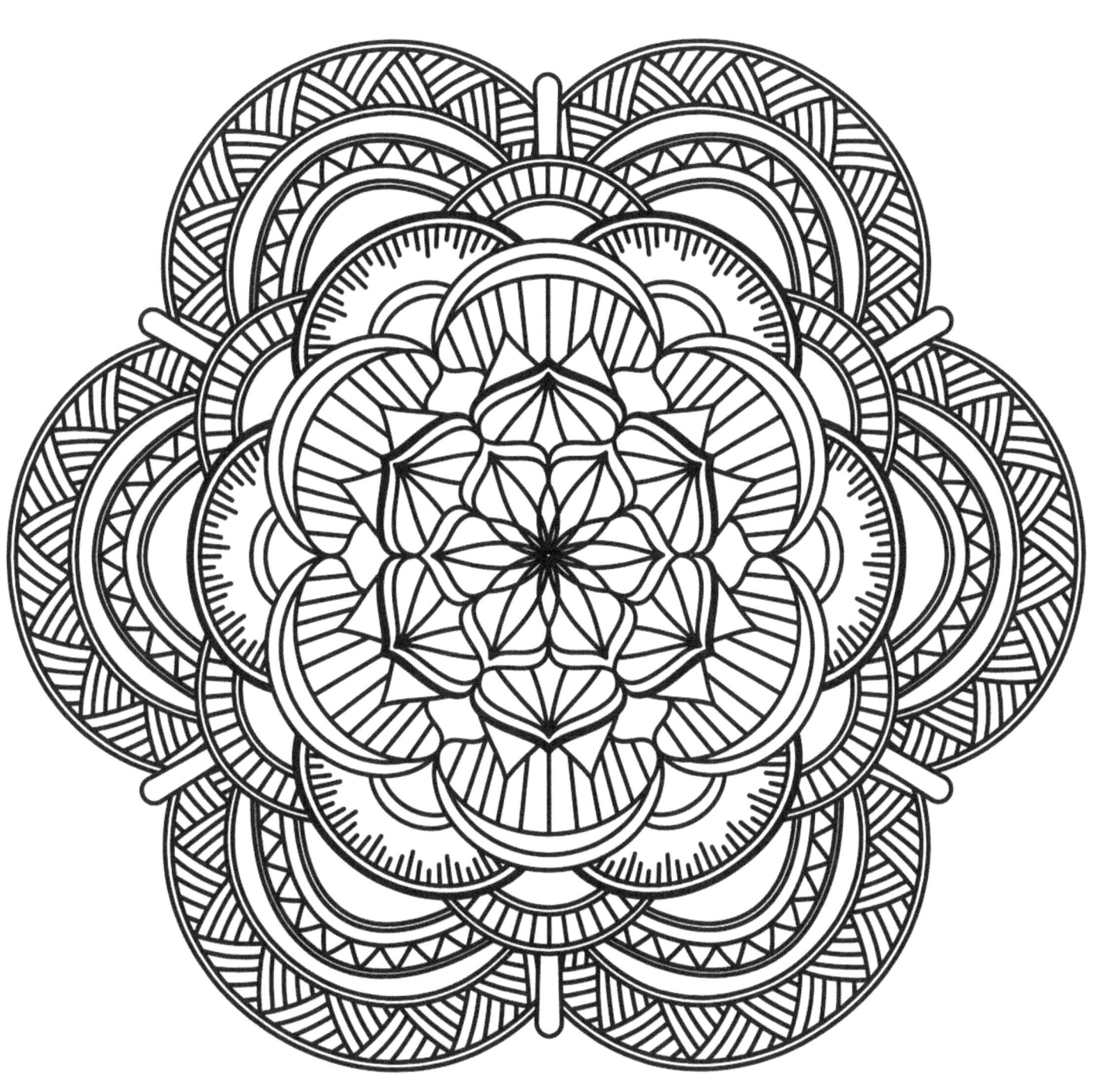

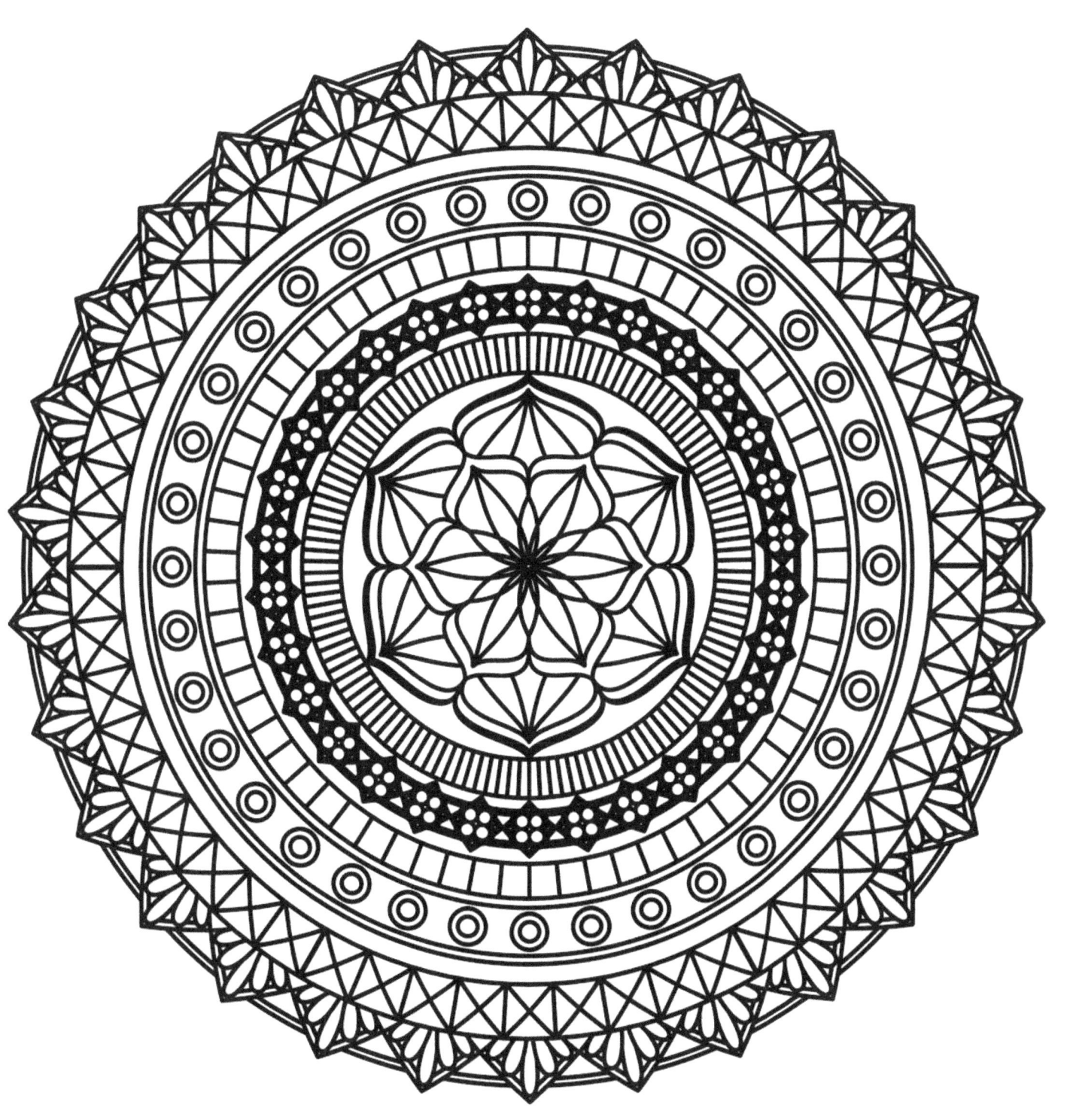

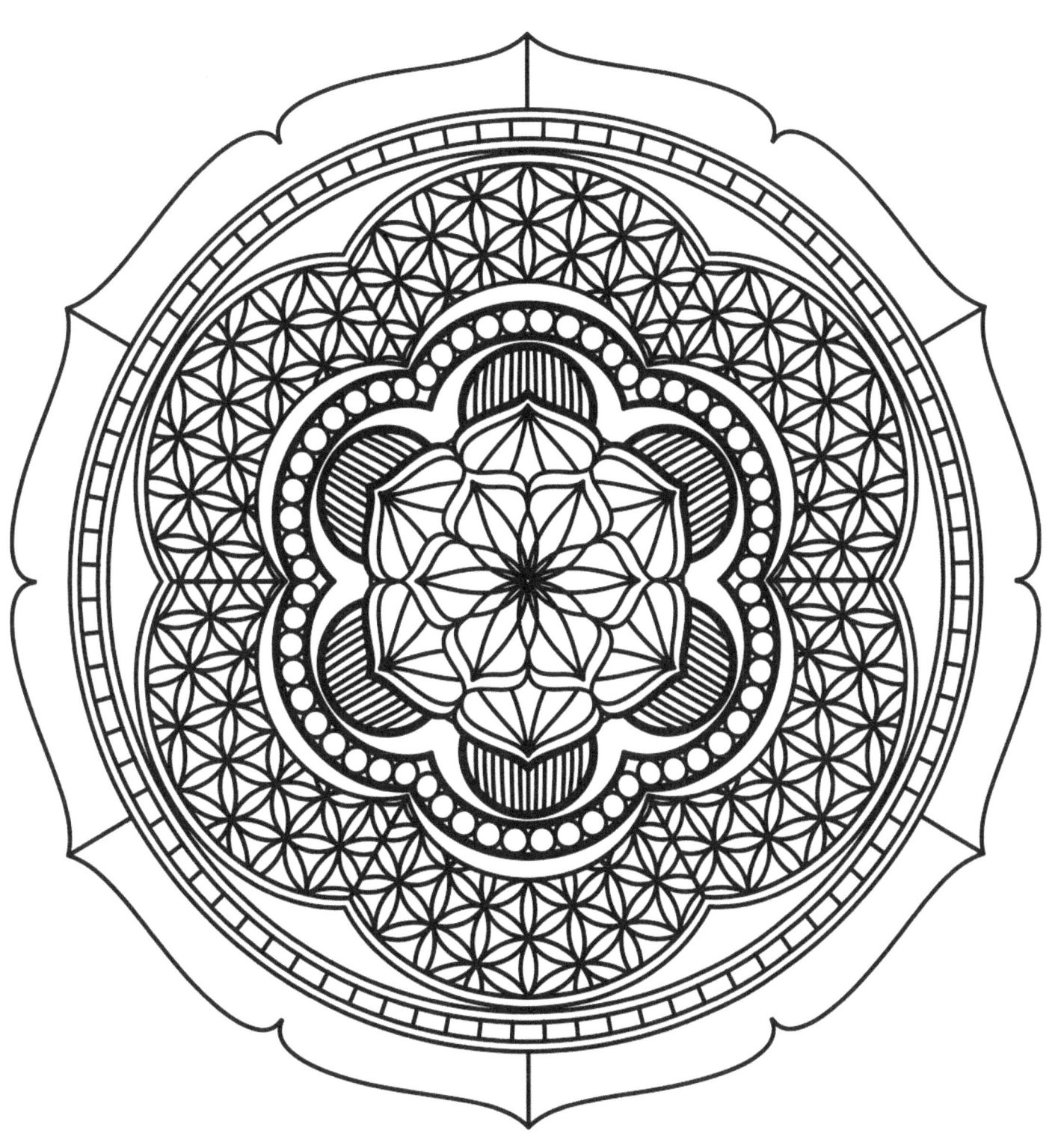

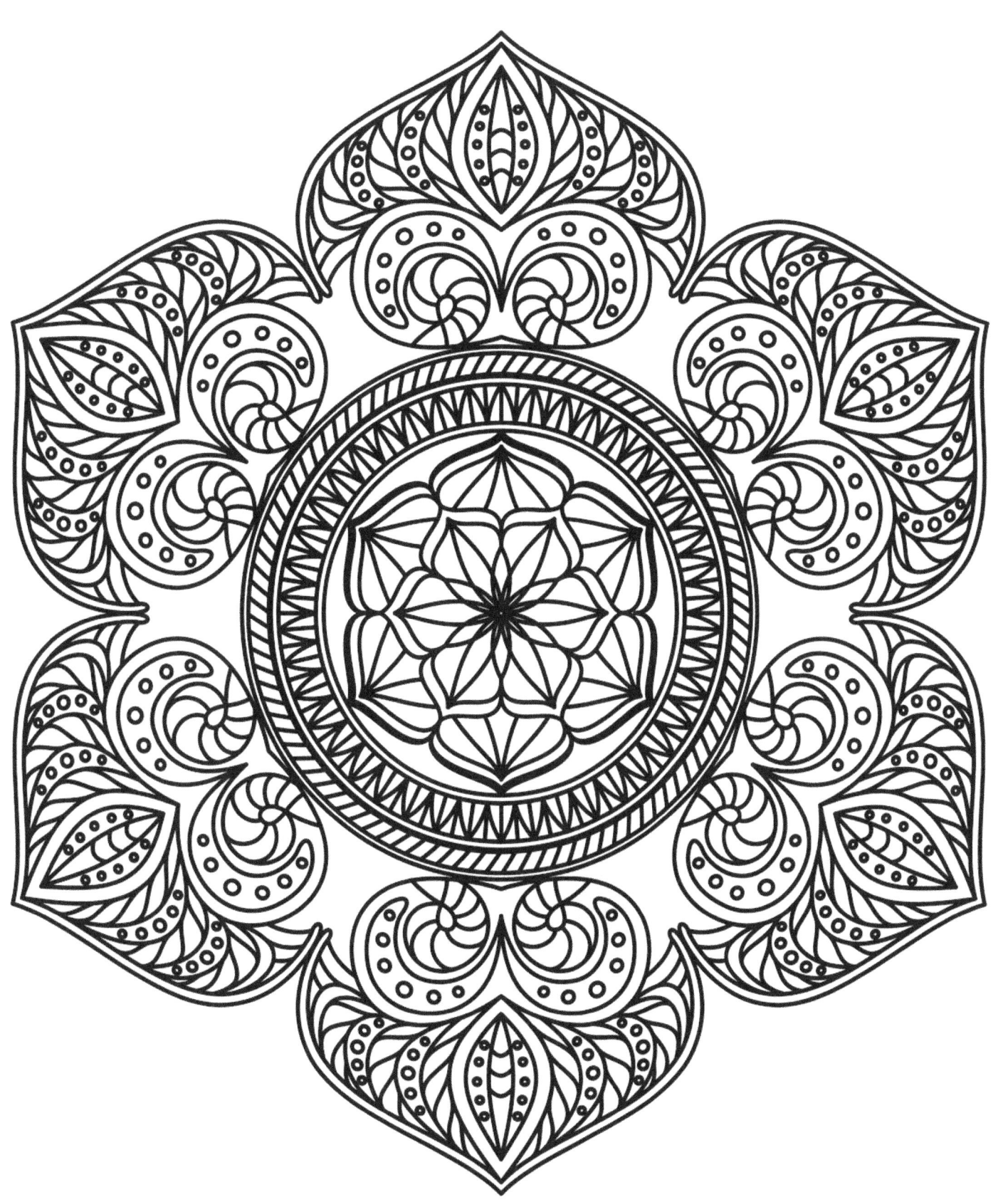

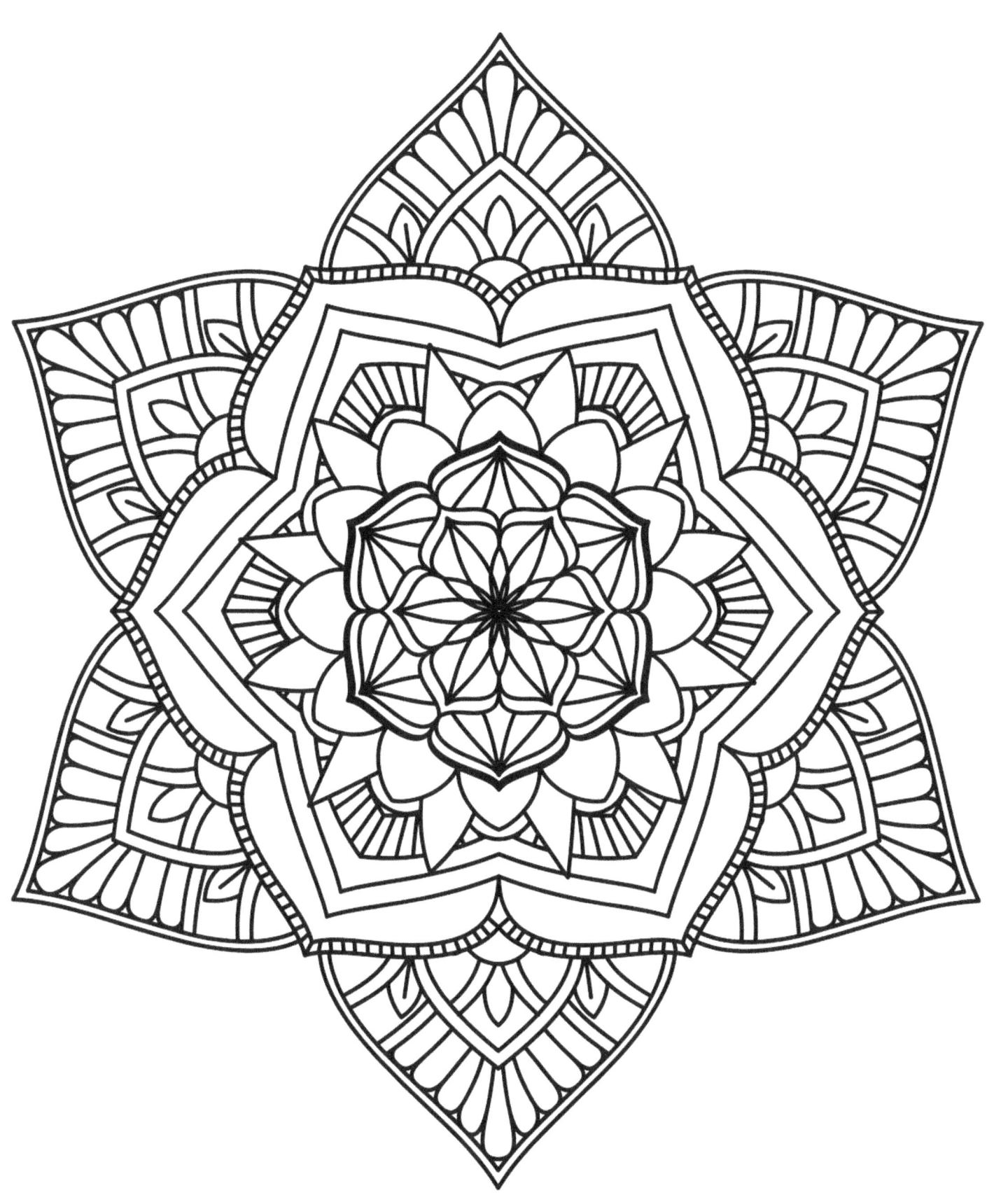

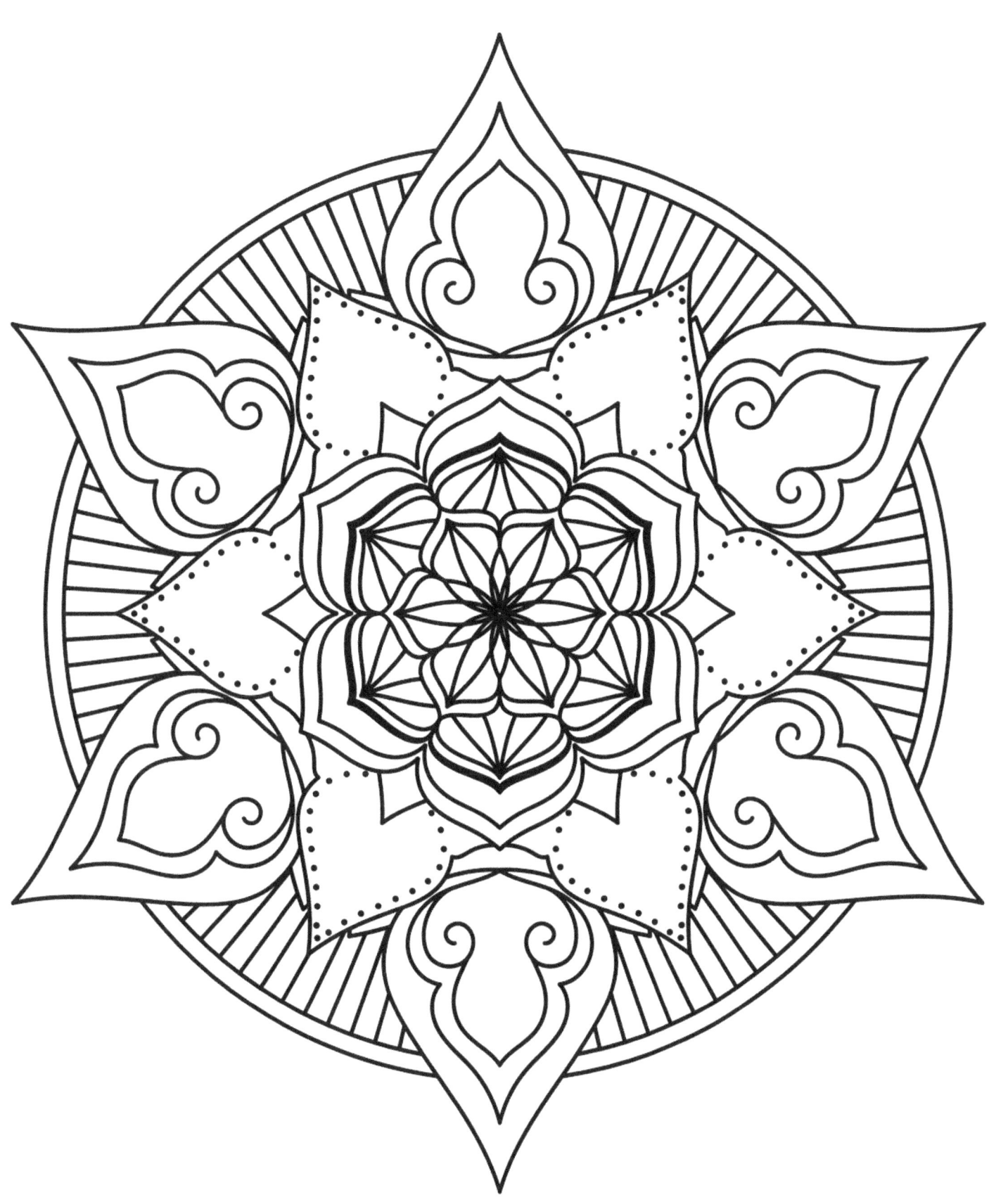

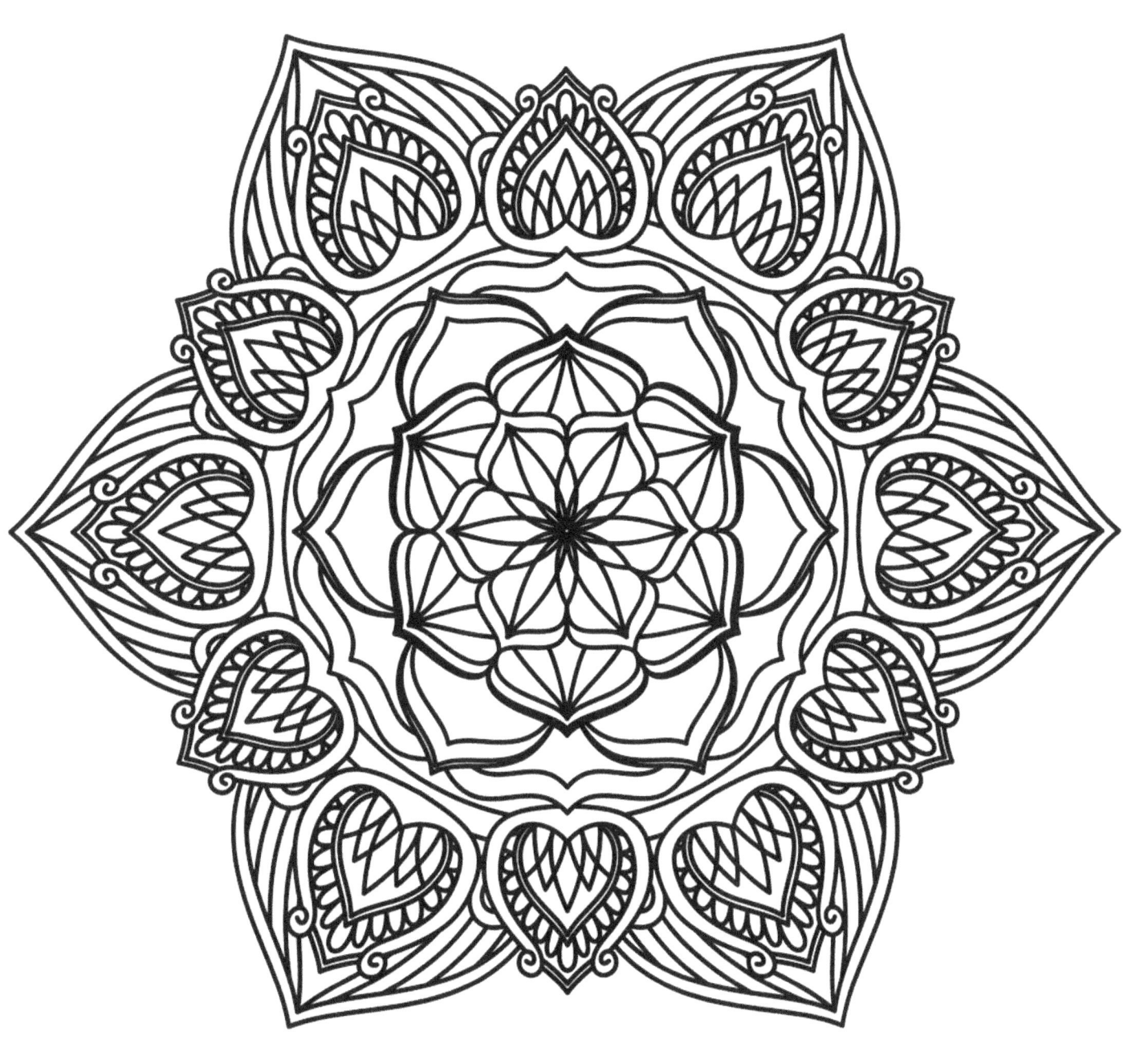

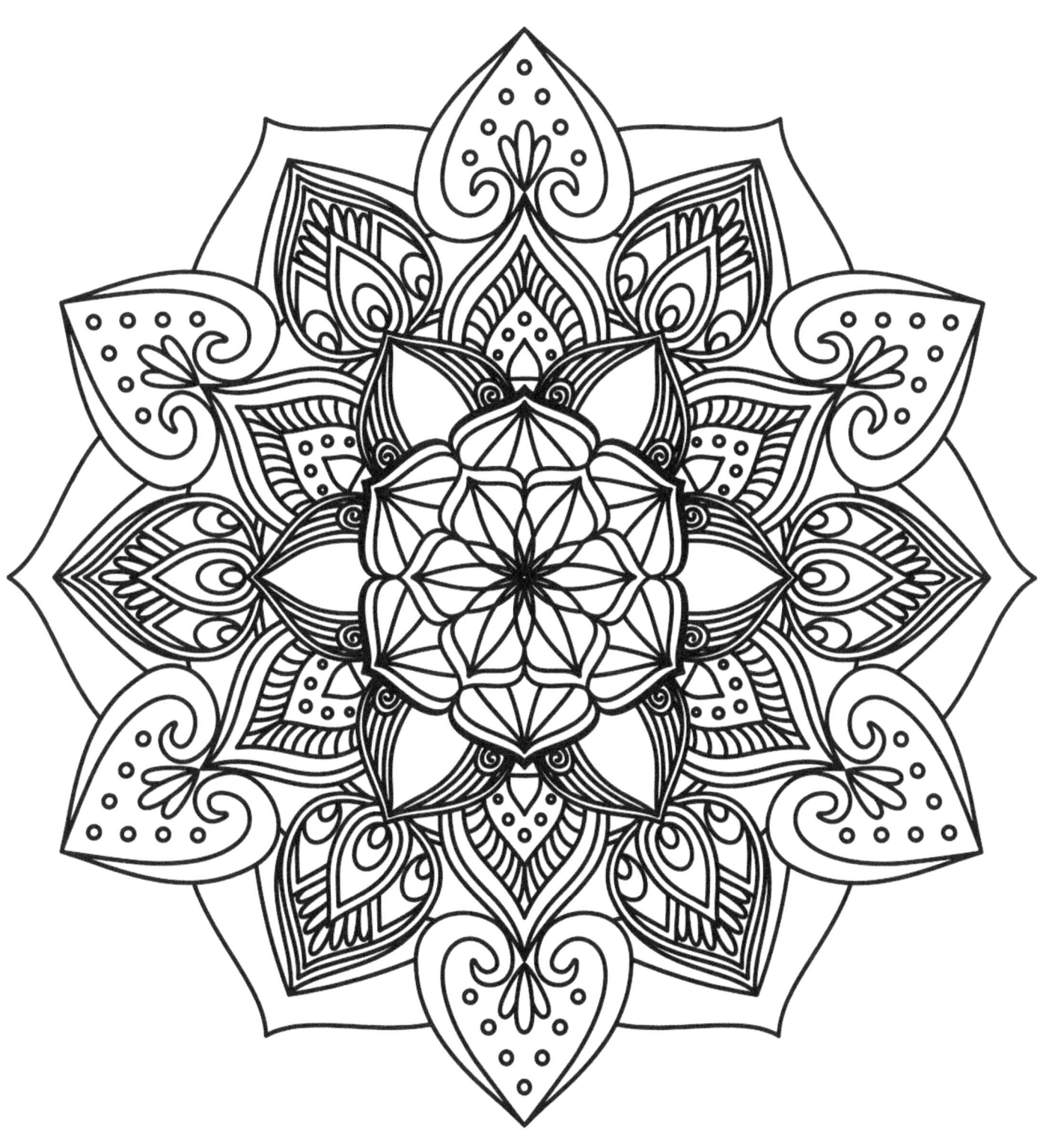

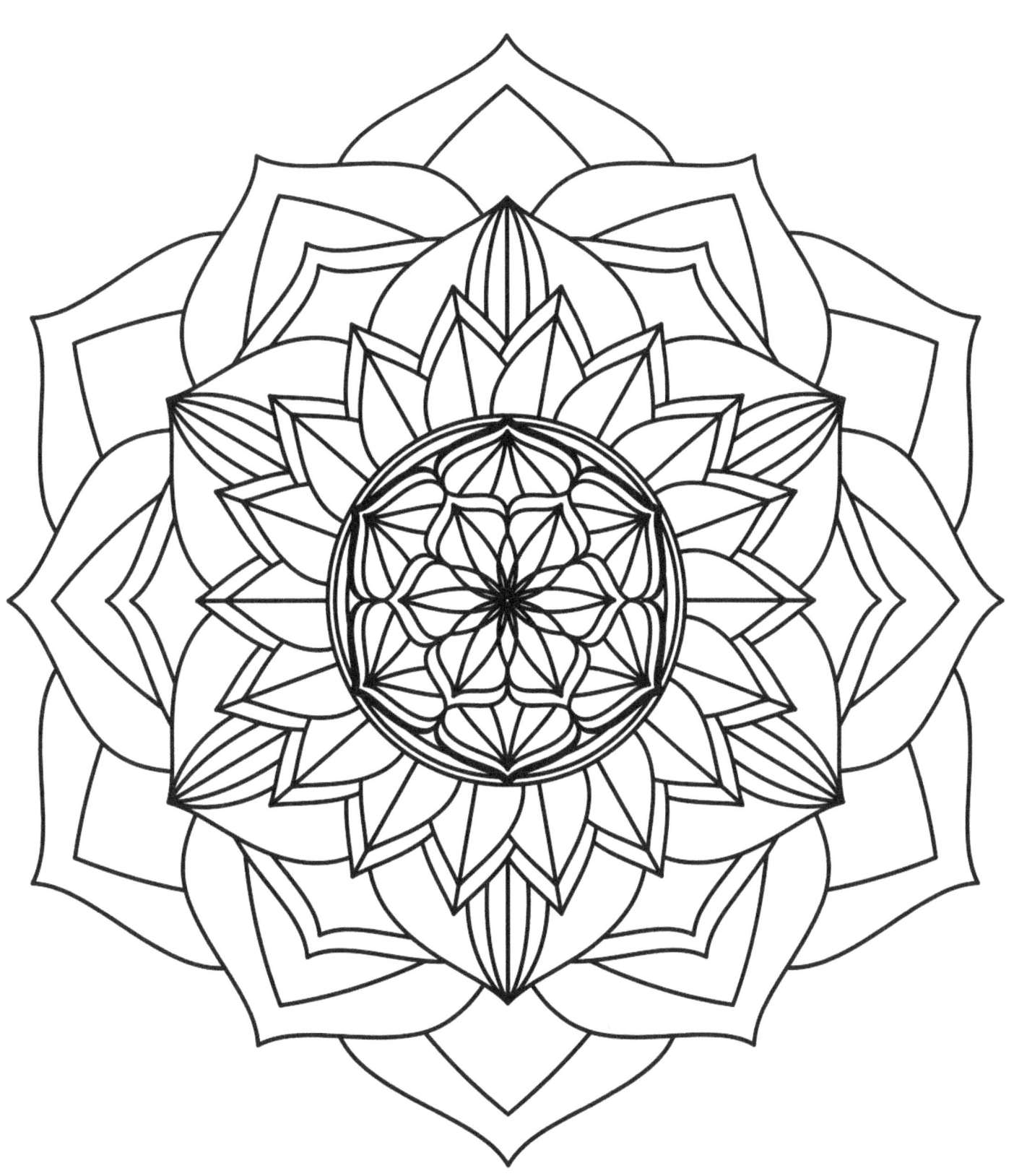

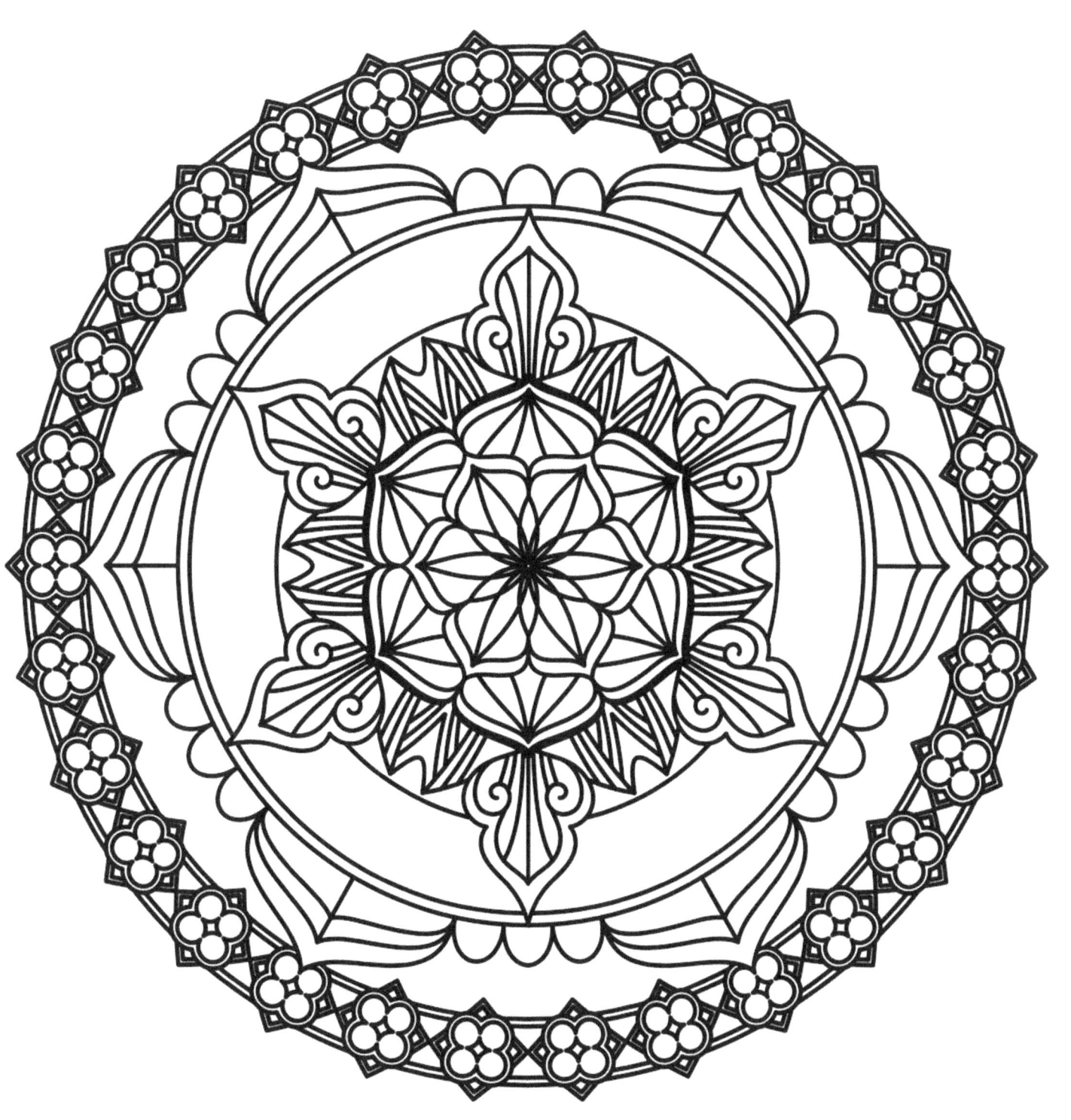

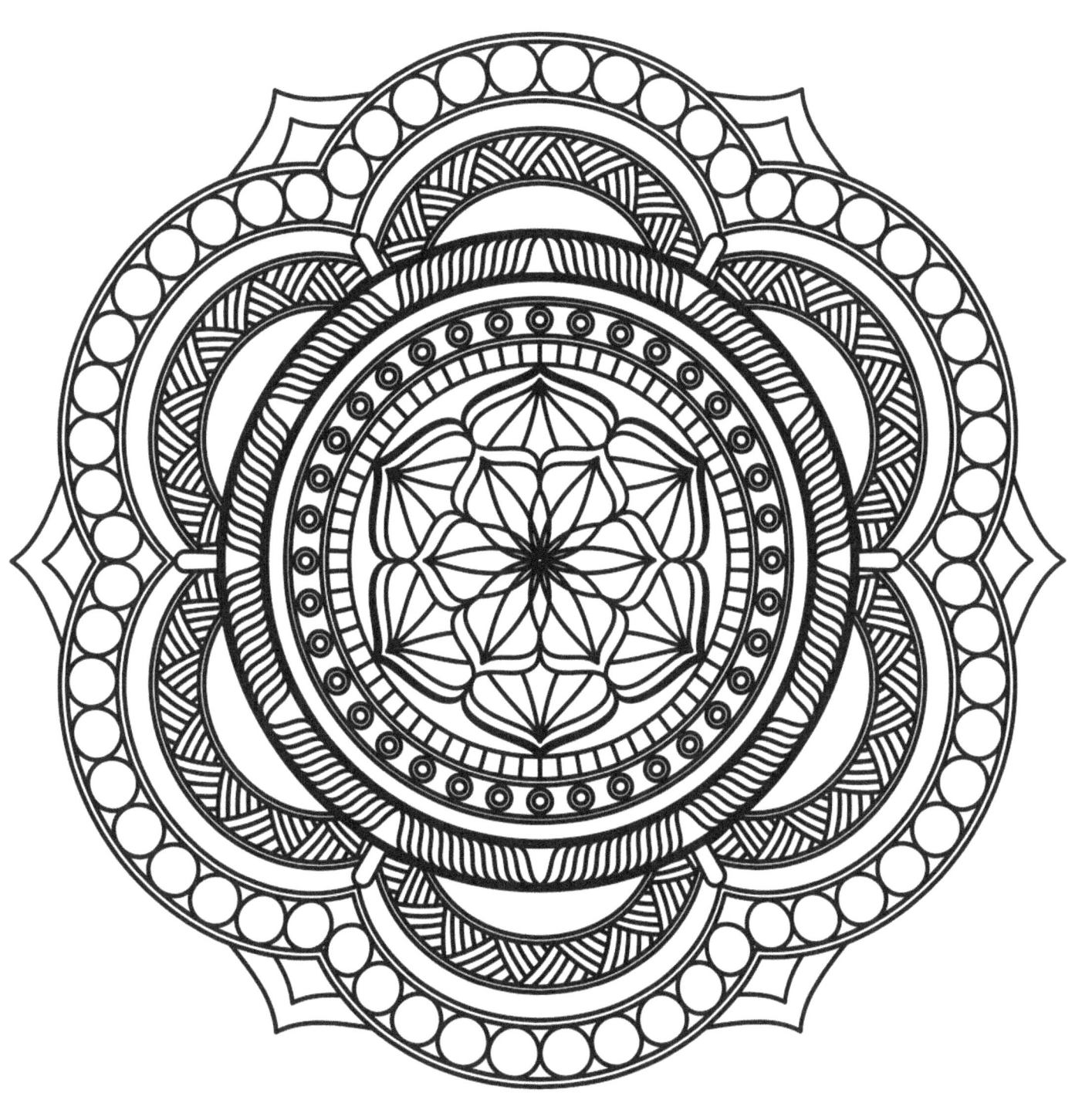

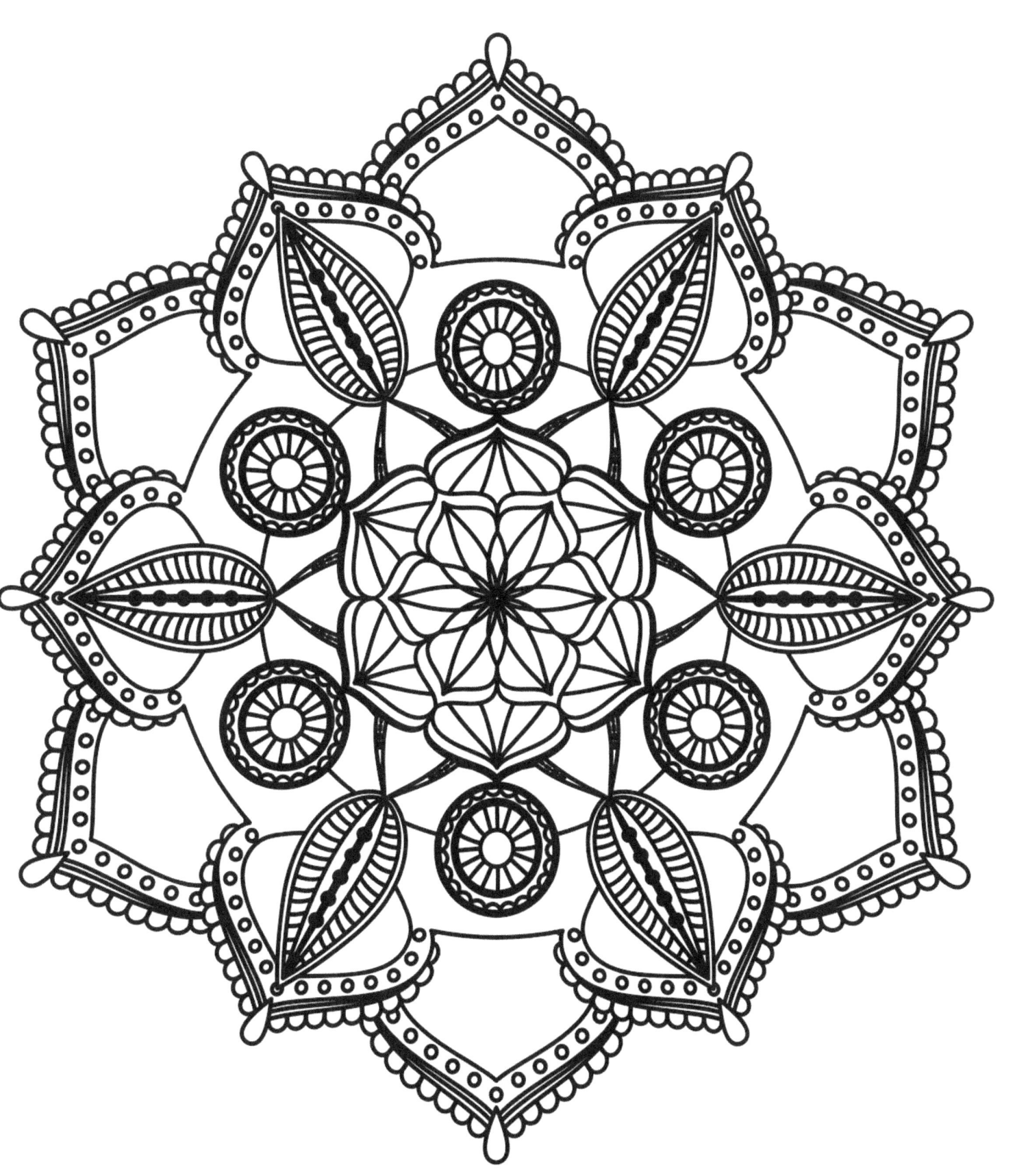

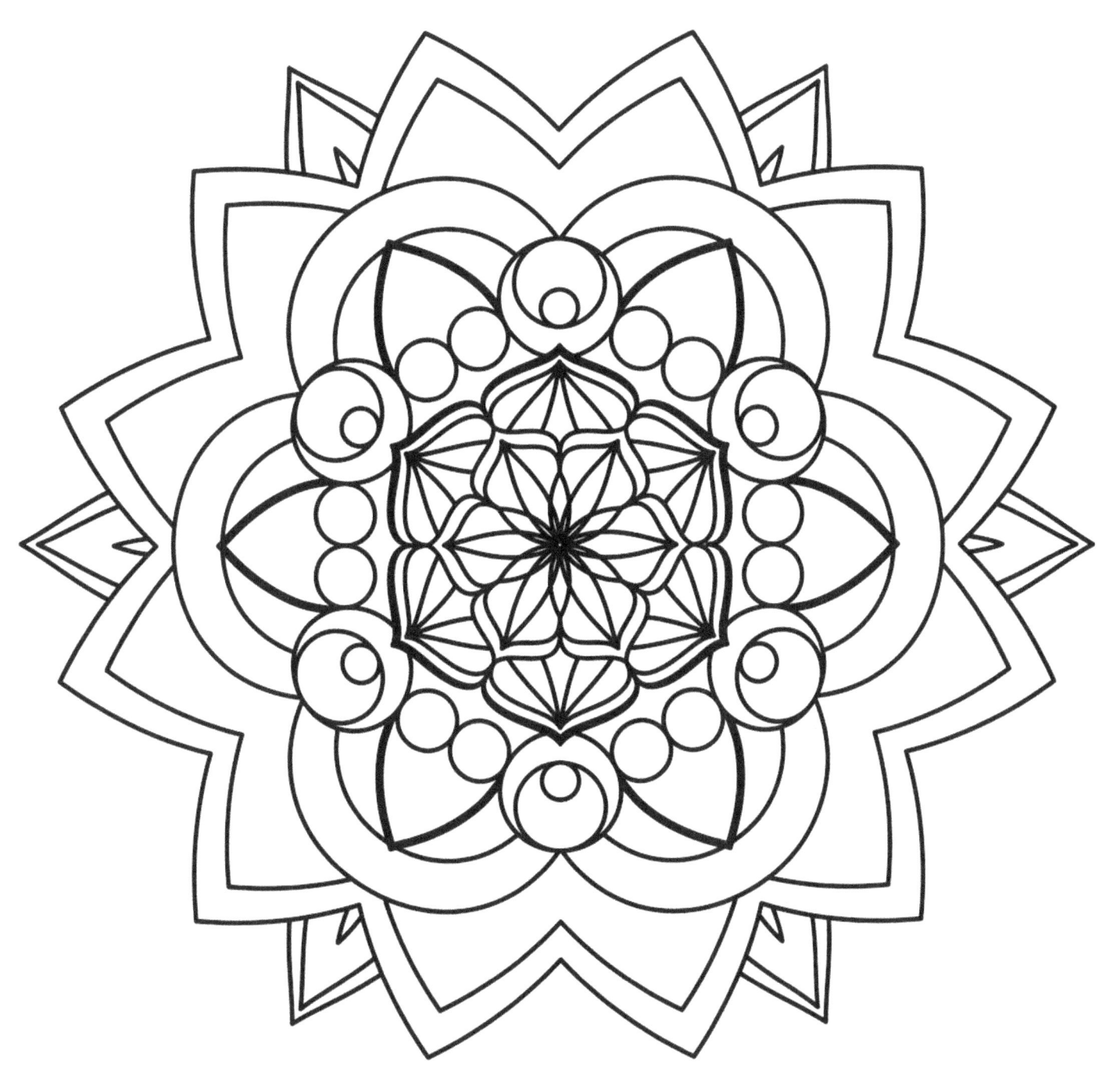